ROYAL COURT
DruidNew

Royal Court Theatre and Druid present

LEAVES

by **Lucy Caldwell**

First performance at Druid Theatre, Chapel Lane, Galway on 1 March 2007.
First performance at the Royal Court Jerwood Theatre Upstairs, Sloane Square, London
on 14 March 2007.

LEAVES

by **Lucy Caldwell**

Phyllis **Fiona Bell**
Poppy **Alana Brennan/Daisy Maguire**
David **Conor Lovett**
Clover **Penelope Maguire**
Lori **Kathy Rose O'Brien**

Director **Garry Hynes**
Set and Costume Designer **Francis O'Connor**
Lighting Designer **Ben Ormerod**
Sound Designer **John Leonard**
Composer **Sam Jackson**
Casting **Maureen Hughes**
Production Manager **Eamonn Fox**
Technical Manager **Barry O'Brien**
Company Stage Manager **Tim Smith**
Stage Manager **Sarah Lynch**
Costume Supervisor **Doreen McKenna**
Carpenter **Gus Dewar**
Graphic Design by **Bite! Associates**

For the Royal Court
Production Manager **Sue Bird**
Stage Manager **Carla Archer**

THE COMPANY

Lucy Caldwell (writer)
Leaves is Lucy's first full-length play, which
won the George Devine Award 2006.

Fiona Bell
Theatre includes: A Month in the Country,
Medea (Abbey, Dublin); How Many Miles to
Babylon (Second Age Theatre Co.);
The Country (Project Arts Theatre);
Dinner with Friends (Guna Nua/Andrews
Lane Production); Pride and Prejudice,
See You Next Tuesday (Gate, Dublin);
Adrenalin Heart (Bush); Animal (The Red
Room/Soho); The Misanthrope (Chichester
Festival Theatre); Henry VI: Parts 1,2 and 3,
Richard III (RSC); Snake (Hampstead);
Cyrano de Bergerac (Communicado/
Almeida); Sacred Hearts (Communicado);
MacBeth, Good, Brilliant Traces,
Mate in Three (Tron); Mirandolina,
The Masterbuilder, Dancing at Lughnasa,
Bedroom Face, Oleanna (Royal Lyceum);
The Lament for Arthur Cleary, Jump the Life
to Come (7.84).
Film and television includes: Gregory's 2
Girls, Trainspotting, Stand and Deliver, I Saw
You, Between Dreams, Mistgate, Afterlife,
East Enders, Casualty, Manhunters, Soldier
Soldier, City Central, A Low Winter Sun,
Doctors, Rockface, Taggart, Truth or Dare,
The Creatives.

Alana Brennan
TV includes: Killanaskully, Northanger Abbey.
Alana is studying Drama and Dance at the
Irish Academy of Performing Arts in
Limerick.

Garry Hynes (director)
For Druid: The Year of the Hiker, Empress of
India (& Dublin Theatre Festival 2006),
DruidSynge (& Dublin/Inis Meain/Edinburgh
International Festival 2005/Minneapolis/
Lincoln Center Festival New York 2006),
Sharon's Grave, Sive, Lovers' Meeting,
Conversations on a Homecoming,
Bailegangaire, The Shaughran, The Wood of
the Whispering.
For the Royal Court (in co-productions
with Druid): On Raftery's Hill, The Beauty
Queen of Leenane, The Lonesome West,

The Leenane Trilogy, Portia Coughlan
(& Abbey, Dublin/Peacock, Dublin).
Other theatre includes: Translations
(Biltmore, New York); King of the Castle,
The Plough and the Stars, The Power of
Darkness, Famine, A Whistle in the Dark;
The Man of Mode, Song of the Nightingale
(RSC); Mr Peters' Connections
(Signature, New York); Crimes of the Heart
(Second, New York); My Brilliant Divorce
(West End); Crestfall (Gate, Dublin);
16 Wounded (Walter Kerr, Broadway);
A Streetcar Named Desire
(Kennedy Center, Washington).
Awards include: In 1998, first woman to
receive a Tony Award for Direction for
The Beauty Queen of Leenane; Irish Times/
ESB Irish Theatre Award for Best Director
2002; Special Tribute Award for contribution
to Irish Theatre 2005.
Garry Hynes founded Druid in 1975 and
worked as its Artistic Director from 1975
to 1991, and from 1995 to date. From 1991
to 1994 she was Artistic Director of the
Abbey Theatre, Dublin.

Sam Jackson (composer)
For Druid: The Year of the Hiker,
DruidSynge (& Dublin/Inis Meain/Edinburgh
International Festival 2005/Minneapolis/
Lincoln Center Festival New York 2006),
The Playboy of the Western World (& Perth,
Australia), The Tinker's Wedding, The Well of
the Saints.
Other theatre includes: Translations
(Biltmore, New York); Yokohama Delegation
(Performance Corporation/Kilkenny Arts
Festival); A Midsummer Night's Dream
(Civic); Twelfth Night (Natural Shocks
Theatre Co.); The Murder Ballads (Kilkenny
Arts Festival); Boy Gets Girl (About Face);
Entertainment (Bedrock).
Awards include: The Walton Memorial
Ensemble Prize 2001 (joint winner);
The Walton Memorial scholarship 2001;
Roland Piano Prize 1999.
Sam has composed and performed widely
for various genres, including dance, film,
cabaret and television. He currently tours as
keyboard player for Moya Brennan of
Clannad.

John Leonard (sound design)
For Druid: The Year of the Hiker, Empress of India (& Dublin Theatre Festival 2006), DruidSynge (& Dublin/Inis Meain/Edinburgh International Festival 2005/Minneapolis/Lincoln Center Festival New York 2006). Other theatre includes: Translations (Biltmore, New York); Flint Street Nativity, The Odd Couple, The Entertainer, Still Life, The Astonished Heart, Ma Rainey's Black Bottom, The Anniversary (Liverpool Playhouse); 2000 Years, Paul, The UN Inspector (National), Jumpers (National/West End/Broadway); Antony and Cleopatra, Much Ado About Nothing, The Prisoner's Dilemma, Romeo & Juliet (RSC); The Old Masters, The Birthday Party (Birmingham Rep/West End); Cinderella, The Dumb Waiter (Oxford Playhouse); The Merry Wives of Windsor, The Merchant of Venice, Cymbeline, Twelfth Night (Ludlow Festival); Beckett, Les Liaisons Dangereuses, Sweet Panic, Absolutely! Perhaps, The Anniversary, Losing Louis, Embers, Smaller, Donkey's Years, Guantánamo (West End), The Master Builder (tour), Private Lives (Broadway); How to Act Around Cops, Flush, Mercy, Colder Than Here (Soho); Midnight's Children (London/tour/New York); Sunday Father, Born Bad, In Arabia We'd All Be Kings (Hampstead); The Best of Friends (tour/West End); The Mercy Seat, I.D., Whistling Psyche, Brighton Rock, Macbeth, Hedda Gabler, The Hypochondriac (Almeida); The Dwarfs (Tricycle); Under Milk Wood (Wales Theatre Co.); Scapino (Chichester); Much Ado About Nothing, Cyrano de Bergerac, Les Liaisons Dangereuses, The Iceman Cometh, Hamlet, Medea, The Judas Kiss, Aristocrats (Broadway); Madame Tussaud's Exhibitions in New York, Warwick Castle and Amsterdam.
Awards include: Drama Desk Award and Sound Designer of the Year awards; Honorary Fellow of The Guildhall School of Music and Drama.
John's book on theatre sound is now in preparation for its second edition.

Conor Lovett
Theatre includes: The Beckett Trilogy (Molloy, Malone Dies, The Unnamable), Texts for Nothing III, VIII & XI, A Piece of Monologue, Waiting for Godot, Rough for Theatre I (Gare St Lazare Players Ireland); Endgame (Stagecraft); What Where, Acts Without Words I & II (Barbican/Gate Beckett Festival 1999); Waiting for Godot (Gate, Dublin/China tour); Waiting for Godot (Rubicon Theatre, Ventura, CA); The Good Thief (Rubicon Theatre/Gare St Lazare Players Ireland); The Three Legged Fool, Banana for the Boy King, Bouncers, Requiem for a Heavyweight, The Homecoming, Marie & Bruce (Gare St Lazare Players Chicago); The Bull (Fabulous Beast Dance Theatre); Orpheus (Steeple Theatre Company); Leonce and Lena (Corcadorca).
Radio includes: Embers, Rough for Radio II, Words and Music, Cascando, All That Fall.
Film and television includes: L'Entente Cordiale, Fallout, Small Engine Repair, Intermission, Moll Flanders, Shut Eye, Fair City, The Kings of Cork City.

Daisy Maguire
Daisy attends drama classes at the Betty Ann Norton Theatre School, Dublin.

Penelope Maguire
Penelope attends drama classes at the Betty Ann Norton Theatre School, Dublin.

Kathy Rose O'Brien
Theatre includes: Widows, Platonov, The Cosmonaut's Last Message to the Woman He Once Loved in the Former Soviet Union (RADA, graduating 2006); The Birthday Party (Bristol Old Vic); What's Their Life Got, Listening Out (Theatre 503).

Francis O'Connor (design)
For Druid: The Year of the Hiker, DruidSynge (& Dublin/Inis Meain/Edinburgh International Festival 2005/Minneapolis/Lincoln Center Festival New York 2006), Empress of India (& Dublin Theatre Festival 2006), The Playboy of the Western World (& Perth, Australia), The Well of the Saints, The Tinker's Wedding, Sharon's Grave, Sive, The Good Father, My Brilliant Divorce (& West End), The Country Boy, The Way You Look Tonight, Shadow and Substance, Wild Harvest.

For the Royal Court (in co-productions with Druid): The Beauty Queen of Leenane, The Lonesome West, The Leenane Trilogy. Other theatre includes: Translations (Biltmore, New York); The Shaughran, The House of Bernarda Alba, The Plough and the Stars, Communion, Iphigenia, Big Maggie, The House, Juno and the Paycock (Abbey, Dublin); Freedom of the City (Abbey, Dublin/New York); The Colleen Bawn, Tarry Flynn (Abbey, Dublin/National); Crestfall (Gate, Dublin); Sixteen Wounded (Walter Kerr, Broadway); Mr. Peters' Connections (Signature, New York). Francis is a regular designer with the Young Vic, Royal Lyceum Edinburgh and Chichester Festival. Awards include: Best Designer in the 1997 and 2000 Irish Times/ESB Irish Theatre Awards.

Ben Ormerod (lighting designer)
For Druid: The Leenane Trilogy, The Country Boy.
Other theatre includes: The Importance of Being Earnest, The Wake, The House, Made in China (Abbey, Dublin/Peacock, Dublin); The Colleen Bawn; Remembrance of Things Past (National); Kvetch (Kilkenny Arts Festival); The Spanish Golden Age season (RSC); Twelfth Night, A Winter's Tale, A Midsummer Night's Dream, Rose Rage (Propeller, all UK/USA); See How They Run, Macbeth (West End).
Opera includes: La Traviata (ENO); Baa Baa Black Sheep (Opera North/BBC2).
Dance includes: Work for Rambert, Cullberg Ballet, Ballet Gulbenkian, Phoenix, Skånes Dansteater and Introdans.
As director, theatre includes: Dimetos (Gate); Kieslowski's Dekalog (E15).

ROYAL COURT BAR & FOOD

MONDAY TO SATURDAY 11AM - 11PM RESERVATIONS 020 7565 5058

THE ENGLISH STAGE COMPANY AT THE ROYAL COURT

The English Stage Company at the Royal Court opened in 1956 as a subsidised theatre producing new British plays, international plays and some classical revivals.

The first artistic director George Devine aimed to create a writers' theatre, 'a place where the dramatist is acknowledged as the fundamental creative force in the theatre and where the play is more important than the actors, the director, the designer'. The urgent need was to find a contemporary style in which the play, the acting, direction and design are all combined. He believed that 'the battle will be a long one to continue to create the right conditions for writers to work in'.

Devine aimed to discover 'hard-hitting, uncompromising writers whose plays are stimulating, provocative and exciting'. The Royal Court production of John Osborne's Look Back in Anger in May 1956 is now seen as the decisive starting point of modern British drama and the policy created a new generation of British playwrights. The first wave included John Osborne, Arnold Wesker, John Arden, Ann Jellicoe, N F Simpson and Edward Bond. Early seasons included new international plays by Bertolt Brecht, Eugène Ionesco, Samuel Beckett and Jean-Paul Sartre.

The theatre started with the 400-seat proscenium arch Theatre Downstairs, and in 1969 opened a second theatre, the 60-seat studio Theatre Upstairs. Some productions transfer to the West End, such as Tom Stoppard's Rock 'n' Roll, My Name is Rachel Corrie, Terry Johnson's Hitchcock Blonde, Caryl Churchill's Far Away and Conor McPherson's The Weir. Recent touring productions include Sarah Kane's 4.48 Psychosis (US tour) and Ché Walker's Flesh Wound (Galway Arts Festival). The Royal Court also co-produces plays which transfer to the West End or tour internationally, such as Conor McPherson's Shining City (with Gate Theatre, Dublin), Sebastian Barry's The Steward of Christendom and Mark Ravenhill's Shopping and Fucking (with Out of Joint), Martin McDonagh's The Beauty Queen Of Leenane (with Druid), Ayub Khan Din's East is East (with Tamasha).

Since 1994 the Royal Court's artistic policy has again been vigorously directed to finding and producing a new generation of playwrights. The writers include Joe Penhall, Rebecca Prichard, Michael Wynne, Nick Grosso, Judy Upton,

photo: Stephen Cummiiskey

Meredith Oakes, Sarah Kane, Anthony Neilson, Judith Johnson, James Stock, Jez Butterworth, Marina Carr, Phyllis Nagy, Simon Block, Martin McDonagh, Mark Ravenhill, Ayub Khan Din, Tamantha Hammerschlag, Jess Walters, Ché Walker, Conor McPherson, Simon Stephens, Richard Bean, Roy Williams, Gary Mitchell, Mick Mahoney, Rebecca Gilman, Christopher Shinn, Kia Corthron, David Gieselmann, Marius von Mayenburg, David Eldridge, Leo Butler, Zinnie Harris, Grae Cleugh, Roland Schimmelpfennig, Chloe Moss, DeObia Oparei, Enda Walsh, Vassily Sigarev, the Presnyakov Brothers, Marcos Barbosa, Lucy Prebble, John Donnelly, Clare Pollard, Robin French, Elyzabeth Gregory Wilder, Rob Evans, Laura Wade, Debbie Tucker Green, Levi David Addai and Simon Farquhar. This expanded programme of new plays has been made possible through the support of A.S.K. Theater Projects and the Skirball Foundation, The Jerwood Charity, the American Friends of the Royal Court Theatre and (in 1994/5 and 1999) the National Theatre Studio.

The refurbished theatre in Sloane Square opened in February 2000, with a policy still inspired by the first artistic director George Devine. The Royal Court is an international theatre for new plays and new playwrights, and the work shapes contemporary drama in Britain and overseas.

The Royal Court's long and successful history of innovation has been built by generations of gifted and imaginative individuals. For information on the many exciting ways you can help support the theatre, please contact the Development Department on 020 7565 5079.

DRUID

Druid Theatre Company was founded in Galway in 1975 by three graduates of NUI Galway, Mick Lally, Marie Mullen and Garry Hynes and its foundation marked the establishment of the first professional theatre company in Ireland outside Dublin. Since then it has been at the forefront of the development of Irish theatre; its regional touring pioneered the Irish touring network and its international success has been unparalleled by any other Irish arts organisation. Recent international touring includes visits to London, Edinburgh, Sydney, Perth, Washington, D.C., Minneapolis and New York. The company has had two artistic directors: Garry Hynes (1975–91 and 1995 to date) and Maeliosa Stafford (1991–94).

Druid has always worked to reinvigorate perceptions of classic dramatic works and to engage with new dramatic work of a challenging, innovative and daring kind. It has drawn extensively from the Irish dramatic repertoire, including acclaimed productions of classics by Dion Boucicault and M.J. Molloy. Productions that have gone on to gain international recognition include The Playboy of the Western World (1982), At the Black Pig's Dyke (1992), Conversations on a Homecoming (1985), and Bailegangaire (1985) featuring Siobhan McKenna in one of her finest dramatic performances. The latter two productions formed part of a major association between Druid and Tom Murphy who was Writer-in-Association with the company and had four of his major works première in Galway.

In 1996 Druid premièred Martin McDonagh's debut work The Beauty Queen of Leenane, in a co-production with the Royal Court Theatre. The Beauty Queen of Leenane opened in Galway and subsequently played in London, Sydney, Dublin, and on Broadway, where the production won four Tony Awards, including Best Director for Garry Hynes, the first woman to win the award. In The Leenane Trilogy (also with the Royal Court) The Beauty Queen of Leenane was joined by premières of McDonagh's A Skull in Connemara and The Lonesome West. Other recent successes include My Brilliant Divorce by Geraldine Aron (a Druid commission that premièred in Galway and was subsequently presented in the West End with Dawn French); and three works by John B. Keane, Sive (2002), Sharon's Grave (2003) and The Year of the Hiker (2006).

DruidSynge, the company's critically acclaimed production of all six of John Millington Synge's plays on the same day, premièred at the Galway Arts Festival in 2005 and has since toured to Dublin, the Edinburgh International Festival, Inis Meáin, the Guthrie Theater in Minneapolis and Lincoln Center Festival New York. A production of The Playboy of the Western World originating in DruidSynge performs at Tokyo International Arts Festival in March 2007. DruidSynge has been described by Charles Isherwood of The New York Times as 'the highlight not just of my theatregoing year but of my theatregoing life' and by The Irish Times as 'one of the greatest achievements in the history of Irish theatre'.

Through its new writing programme, DruidNew, Druid premièred two new plays in 2006, The Walworth Farce by Enda Walsh and Empress of India by Stuart Carolan and consistently commissions, develops, and produces new plays by a wide range of emerging and established writers both from Ireland and abroad.

Patron **Mary McAleese,** President of Ireland
(Éarlamh **Máire Mhic Ghiolla Íosa,** Uachtarán na hÉireann)

Board **Séamus O'Grady** (Chairman),
Tarlach de Blácam, Donncha O'Connell, Eugene O'Kelly, Breda Ryan, Donal Shiels Founders **Garry Hynes, Mick Lally, Marie Mullen**

FOR DRUID
Artistic Director **Garry Hynes**
Acting Managing Director **Felicity O'Brien**
Financial Controller **Bernie Harrigan**
Administrator **Sinéad McPhillips**
New Writing Manager **Thomas Conway**
Administration Assistants **Carmel Curley and Shona McCarthy**

Druid wishes to thank Outgoing Managing Director Fergal McGrath.

ACKNOWLEDGEMENTS
Druid wishes to express its continuing gratitude to Thomas McDonagh & Company Ltd. for their support of the company and gratefully acknowledges the assistance of Galway City Council and Galway County Council.

 Druid is grant-aided by The Arts Council of Ireland An Chomhairle Ealaíon

 Druid gratefully acknowledges the assistance of Culture Ireland.

PROGRAMME SUPPORTERS

The Royal Court (English Stage Company Ltd) receives its principal funding from Arts Council England, London. It is also supported financially by a wide range of private companies, charitable and public bodies, and earns the remainder of its income from the box office and its own trading activities.

The Genesis Foundation supports the Royal Court's work with International Playwrights.

The Artistic Director's Chair is supported by a lead grant from The Peter Jay Sharp Foundation, contributing to the activities of the Artistic Director's office. Over the past nine years the BBC has supported the Gerald Chapman Fund for directors.

ROYAL COURT

A National Theatre of Scotland production

28 March – 21 April
Jerwood Theatre Downstairs

THE WONDERFUL WORLD OF DISSOCIA
by **Anthony Neilson**

direction **Anthony Neilson**
design **Miriam Buether**
lighting design **Chahine Yavroyan**
sound design/composition **Nick Powell**
featuring the original cast

Lisa Jones is on a journey. It's a colourful and exciting off-kilter trip in search of one lost hour that has tipped the balance of her life. The inhabitants of the wonderful world she finds herself in – Dissocia – are a curious blend of the funny, the friendly and the brutal. As Neilson himself puts it, 'If you like Alice in Wonderland but there's not enough sex and violence in it, then Dissocia is the show for you'.

Produced originally for the 2004 Edinburgh International Festival, The Wonderful World of Dissocia wowed critics and audiences alike.

This is a hugely original play, both magical and moving, that confirmed Anthony Neilson as one of the major voices in contemporary British theatre.

BOX OFFICE 020 7565 5000
BOOK ONLINE
www.royalcourttheatre.com

Lucy Caldwell
Leaves

faber and faber

First published in 2007
by Faber and Faber Limited
3 Queen Square, London WC1N 3AU

Typeset by Country Setting, Kingsdown, Kent CT14 8ES
Printed in England by Bookmarque, Croydon, Surrey

A CIP record for this book
is available from the British Library

ISBN 978-0-571-23633-6

2 4 6 8 10 9 7 5 3 1

In memoriam
Daphne Moore

and for
Níamh Louise McKee
1990–2005

www.niamhlouisefoundation.com

Acknowledgements

Leaves was written at the National Theatre Studio during the autumn–winter of 2005, and I would like to thank Lucy Davies and all at the Studio, as well as Jack Bradley, Chris Campbell and everyone in the National Theatre's Literary Department. Thanks also to Natalie Abrahami, who guided the play through its first readings and rewrites; to Thomas Conway, Garry Hynes, Felicity O'Brien and the rest of the Druid Theatre Company; to Alan Brodie and Harriet Pennington-Legh; and, at a much earlier stage, to Simon Stephens and the Royal Court YWP; to James Macdonald; also to my 'Doghouse' boys: Nick Harrop, Ben Musgrave, Matt Morrison, Robin Booth, Amman Paul Singh Brar (and Jenny Tuckett). And above all, my most heartfelt thanks to Ben Jancovich and Graham Whybrow, both of whom have been not only wonderful mentors but great friends.

Characters

David
late forties

Phyllis
late forties

Lori
nineteen

Clover
fifteen

Poppy
eleven

Setting

Belfast, present day

Act One

SCENE ONE

The living/dining room.
  It is the evening before Lori is due to return home.
  David, Phyllis, Clover and Poppy are sitting around the table, eating dinner.
  David is eating mechanically. Phyllis is eating quickly and defiantly. Clover is pushing food around her plate and Poppy is not even pretending to eat.
  They are sitting in silence and not meeting each other's eyes.
  The room should feel too big and echoey.
  There is a small pile of gaudily wrapped presents on the floor.
  Silence.

Poppy (*suddenly – she has been trying unsuccessfully to catch someone's eye for a while*) This time tomorrow.

  Beat.

I said, this time tomorrow.

David Yes, Poppy.

Poppy Imagine.

Clover Poppy.

Poppy What?
  Mum.
  This time tomorrow, Mum.

Phyllis Yes, love.

Poppy Are you excited, Clovey?

Clover Shh.

Poppy Why?

David Poppy.

Poppy What?

David That's enough.

Poppy *What?*
I was only *saying.* I was only trying to –

Clover Leave it, / Pops.

Poppy But –

Clover Just leave it.

Silence.

Phyllis There's more bread, if anyone . . .

Clover No thank you.

Phyllis There's almost half a loaf left, I can cut some more.
David?

David I'm all right for the moment, thank you.

Silence.

Poppy (*sulkily*) I was just trying to cheer everyone up, that's all.

Clover Are you not right in the head or something?

David Clover.

Poppy Yeah, *Clover.*

David That applies to you too, Poppy.
Now eat your dinner, come on.

Poppy I'm not hungry any more.

Phyllis Please, Poppy.

Poppy I said I'm not hungry.

David Your mother has gone to the trouble of cooking you your dinner and you'll damn well eat it.

Clover Just eat it, Pops.

Poppy But –

Silence.

You know it's funny but *I* seem to be the only one in this family that cares about her coming home. I've made her a welcome home card. I don't see anyone else making an effort.

Silence.
   Phyllis stops eating abruptly. David carries on eating and does not raise his head. Clover jerks round and glares at Poppy. Poppy ignores her.

And I was the one that wrapped the presents.

Clover Which is a stupid idea anyway what are we giving her *presents* for does anyone really think that she'll actually want /

Phyllis Please, Clover.

Clover What.

Phyllis You're not helping.

Clover *What?* I've just been sitting here trying to eat my dinner *Poppy's* the one who's been /

Poppy I haven't done anything! All I was trying to do was /

David Both of you! You're as bad as each other, would both of you just /

Clover Oh great, so I'm getting blamed as much as *her* now. That's great, that's just /

Phyllis (*loudly, to David*) How was your day, David, did you have a productive day?

David Fine, it was fine, thank you.

Phyllis Good, that's –

   Silence.

Clover (*sadly*) So how was your audition Clover oh my audition it was great thanks Mum thanks for asking /

Phyllis / Your audition . . .

Clover You completely forgot, didn't you?

Phyllis It was today.
   I'm sorry, pet.

   Beat.

Well, how did it go?

   Beat.

Clover *What?*
   I can't believe you /

David / Clover.

Clover / just asked me that, Mum!

David Your mother was only trying to /

Clover Well, if you really want to know it was terrible, it was the worst audition I've ever done and I'm not going to get into the orchestra now so that's that /

Phyllis / Clover –

Clover and I don't want to talk about it any more.

   Silence.

I wasn't going to say anything, I was just seeing if you'd remember. It was the most important audition I've ever done and /

Phyllis I am so sorry, love.

Clover Yeah, well, sorry doesn't make it any better, does it?

Beat.
Phyllis gets up abruptly and leaves.
Silence.

Poppy See what you've done?

Clover See what *I've* done?

Beat.
David hurls his cutlery to the table and gets up and walks out (in a different direction from Phyllis).

Poppy You made Mum cry. Why did you have to say anything anyway? It wasn't Mum's fault she forgot.

Clover (*standing up*) Nothing's anyone's fault, is it.

Clover marches out of the room. Poppy is left sitting on her own.

SCENE TWO

Later on that evening.
Lori's room.
A typical enough teenage bedroom. But it must have a half-hearted feel: much of the childish paraphernalia is gone – but it is not quite an adult room. Posters. Pages ripped from fashion magazines. Photo collages on the walls – many of them of Lori and Clover. Occasional gaps where pictures have been removed. Bookshelves. A couple of trophies or medals. A few soft toys on the top shelf. Knick-knacks. Fairy lights around the window.

A couple of cardboard boxes: Phyllis has been tidying the room; after Lori left for university she intended to paint and redecorate it, but never quite got around to it.
A couple of piles of children's books on the floor.
The curtains are open. The bed is stripped of sheets. Clover is sitting on the bed, knees hunched up in front of her, gazing at the photo collages. The fairy lights are switched on, but the main lights are not.
Phyllis enters and switches on the main lights. Clover starts.

handwritten: 1) Hiding Away.

Clover Mum. *— handwritten:* like a question...

Phyllis I've been looking all over the house for you.

Clover Oh. *— handwritten:* trails off.

Phyllis Been looking everywhere.

Clover Right. Well. *handwritten:* short.   *handwritten:* INNER MONOLOGUE
  Here I am.] *handwritten:* → hesitation but sits.
Phyllis Can I sit down?] *handwritten:* 2) AWKWARD.

Clover shrugs. Phyllis perches on the edge of the bed.
Beat. *handwritten:* turns away.

Phyllis (*lightly*) What are you doing? *handwritten:* 3) Small talk.

Clover Nothing.

Silence. *handwritten:* Starts to turn
Nothing, just *handwritten:* looks into her mum's eyes
  Nothing.] *handwritten:* quickly turns back
Silence. *handwritten:* again.

Phyllis I'm sorry, Clover. *handwritten:* 4) Apologies
Clover It's okay. *handwritten:* grabs hand
              handwritten: shakes it off.
Phyllis No, Clover, it isn't okay. I'm sorry.

→ turns quickly very apologetic.

Clover I'm sorry too. I shouldn't've said anything, Mum. (*Sadly.*) You've got more important things to worry about.

Phyllis No, Clover!
You mustn't think like that, sweetheart.
You are just as important to me.

Silence.

Will you come here (and) let me give you a cuddle?

Clover Mum. – *turns back*

Phyllis Come on. *→ snappy.*

Clover Mu-um. Just – leave it, okay?
→ Clover to Mum her.
Silence. *→ still awkward.*
After a bit Phyllis gets up and walks over to the
window. She stares out for a second. Then she turns
back to the room. She bends down and picks up one of
the story books: a collected Hans Christian Andersen.
She sits down and takes the book in her lap. Strokes
the cover with one finger. Opens it, and riffles through
the pages. Smiles to herself – despite herself.

Phyllis (*suddenly*) 'The first dog, who guarded the chest
of copper shillings, had eyes as big as teacups. The
second dog, who guarded the chest of silver coins –'

Clover / Ohh –   *5) Blast from the past*

Phyllis '– had eyes as big as . . .?'

Beat. *Builds up –*

'Pinwheels. And the third dog, who guarded the chest of
gold –'

Clover Had eyes as big as round towers!   *(get excited)*

Phyllis 'Had eyes as big as round towers.'

Clover 'The Tinder-Box'!

→ forgetting themselves.

Inner Monologue!

15

Phyllis 'The Tinder-Box', that's right.

Clover And – and Dad always used to say it was a warning against playing with matches.

Phyllis So he did!

Clover 'The Tinder-Box'. God.
That's a – a blast from the past.

Phyllis is still riffling through the pages.

Phyllis Listen.
Listen to this one.

Clover Mum, I don't think –

Phyllis 'Peacefully the wide sea lay abroad. No movement could be felt on board our ship.'

Clover Mum, listen to me, Mum, I don't think –

Phyllis (*continuing*) 'The youngest of the monks was very handsome, with a pale melancholy face. He told me that since his sixteenth year he had not seen his mother, who was very dear to him. "And now I shall not see her till we meet in Heaven!" he sighed.'

She stops abruptly.

Clover Mum –

Phyllis It's funny, isn't it, but I can't recall ever reading you this one.

She turns the pages.

Did I ever read it to you, do you remember?

Clover I don't know, Mum.
Probably not, no. Because it's a true one, isn't it, and we never liked the true ones much. It was the fairytales we liked.

Phyllis Yes, perhaps you're right.]

Beat.

[handwritten: not listening to Clover]

[handwritten: 9) Lightening the mood.]

[There's a lovely line in it – listen – where is it – (*Riffling.*)
here it is, here it is: 'It seemed as if men were walking
about with torches at the bottom of the sea, and as if
these were suddenly blazing up.' Isn't that lovely now?]

Clover Yeah but, Mum –   *[handwritten: 10) Taking the lead.]*
(*Sudden resolve.*) I really don't think you should –
Mum, I don't think it helps.
I think what you should do is –
I think the best thing to do is –   *[handwritten: Stand up.]*
To put the books back up in the attic where they came
from.
Mum.   *[handwritten: Shouting *]*
D'ye hear me, Mum? D'ye hear what I'm saying?
Because –

Phyllis Oh, Clover.
What's to be done, eh?]

Beat.

[handwritten: 11) Reality]   *[handwritten: Clover: inner monologue]*

[D'you know, this morning I bumped into the mother of
a girl that went to primary school with Lori. And she
didn't – know, of course, and she said, being polite, 'So
how's Lori getting on?' and I said – I mean I just couldn't
– I couldn't bring myself to – and I just said, 'Good,
good, she's grand.' I mean, what was I supposed to say?   *[handwritten: *]*

Clover Yeah. I don't know.] *[handwritten: – Sit back down.]*

Beat.   *[handwritten: 12) Understanding]*

[**Phyllis** I'm sorry, love.

Clover No, Mum (it's all right) –] *[handwritten: trails off.]*

Beat.

17

change in tense

Hey – look Mum, d'ye want a hand tidying, because, because we could do it now, I mean –

   Beat.

Phyllis It's getting late, love. I think you should go to bed.

Clover What? – *confused*.

Phyllis School tomorrow and all that.

never looks at clover now.

Clover But – if I gave you a hand and that – it wouldn't take long – *really trying*.

Phyllis Thank you love, but –

   Beat.

Clover Mum – *walks out angry.*

She doesn't say what she was going to say. She stands for a second then leaves the room. Phyllis remains with the book on her lap, staring at it.

SCENE THREE

The living room.
   Poppy is under the dining-room table. The story of Peter Pan *is open beside her. She is holding a jotter which she closes and hides behind her back. She freezes and tries to make herself as small as possible.*
   Clover has just come in.

Clover Don't think that because you're under the table I can't see you.
   Don't think that you can hide from me.
   What are you doing under there, anyway?

   Silence.

18

I asked you a question, dickhead.

Silence.

You're so weird, Poppy. You know, if you're not careful you're going to grow up to be really, really weird.

Clover bends down.

Oh my God. You're reading *Peter Pan*.
Peter Pan is a kiddies' book, Poppy, in case you didn't know.
God. You weirdo.

Beat.

Poppy Mum was reading it to me. It was sort of nice. It was like being little again.

Clover You shouldn't encourage Mum.

Poppy It wasn't my idea. I was just helping.

Clover Encouraging Mum doesn't help anyone, Poppy. And you can't let her treat you like you're little. You're not. You're almost twelve, for God's sake. It's unhealthy.

Silence.

I need to talk to you, Poppy. Come out of under there.

Poppy I don't want to.

Clover What?

Poppy I don't want to.

Clover God, you're weird.
I could tell the boys in your class at school.
Is that what you want me to do, Poppy?

Beat.

God, Poppy.

Beat.

Mum's still in Lori's room.
  And Dad's smoking in the garage.

Beat.

Does that mean anything to you, Poppy?
  Does any of that mean anything to you?
  It's so pathetic the way you're acting as if you're the only one.

Beat.

It really is.

Beat.

What are you writing?

Beat.

Give me.

Poppy No.

Clover Give it to me.

Poppy No.

Clover *Give it to me now.*

  She snatches the jotter from Poppy.
    Poppy does not move.
    Clover begins to flick through the pages.

Poppy Give it back.

Beat.

Please, Clovey.
  Please give it back.
  I'm sorry.

Beat.

Clover 'A list of *reasons*'?

Poppy I'm sorry, Clover.

Clover 'We didn't phone her enough.'
   'We should have visited.'
   Why have you written all of this down?
   That isn't even how you spell 'suicide' anyway, stupid.

   She breaks off.
      Beat.

God, Poppy!
   Here. There'd better not be anything I said in here.
I mean it. What I say is my business and it's not to go in
your stupid little diary. All right?

Poppy Words don't belong to anyone.

Clover What?
   I'm warning you, Poppy. You're not to write down
anything that I say or do in here, okay?

   Beat.

I said –

Poppy *Okay*, Clover. Okay.

Clover 'Cause, God, Pops.
   Mum'd better not see this.
   I'm serious, Poppy.

   Silence.

'There's no smoke without fire.'
   What is that supposed to mean?

   Beat.

Poppy It's –
   There's no smoke without fire is what Mum said.
   It was just afterwards, after the phone call, when she

21

and Dad had that big argument about who was to blame.
When Dad said that no one. And Mum said –
    That was what Mum said.
    And then Dad said –

Clover 'Big fish, small pond.'

Poppy Yeah. Big fish, small pond syndrome.

Clover Which is a stupid thing to say anyway. And I
don't think it's true. I think Lori would've been as clever
as any of them.

Poppy Yeah.
    Me too.

    Beat.

Clovey.
    Imagine, right, imagine what it would feel like if she
was dead.

Clover Why?

Poppy (*thrown*) Well, just imagine.
    What would it be like.
    'Cause I keep on trying to imagine, but I can't.

Clover Well –
    Well, if that's what you 'keep on trying to imagine'
then you're stupid, Poppy.
    Because she wouldn't be – dead.
    No way.

    Silence.

Poppy Don't cry, Clovey.

Clover (*fiercely*) *I'm not crying.*

Poppy I cry sometimes, too. Everyone does. Even Dad.
That's why he goes to the garage, so no one can see him,
and he thinks no one knows.

Silence.

It's all right, Clovey.
  Things are going to be all right.

Clover How can they be, Poppy? How can they ever be?

Poppy They will.

  Silence.

Clover Hey Pops, can I come in under there with you?

Poppy What?

Clover See what the room looks like from there?
  Well, can I?

  Poppy stares at her.
    Clover waits for a second then kneels down and crawls in underneath the table. The two sisters sit side by side, not looking at each other.

It does look different from here, doesn't it.

Poppy Yeah.
  That's why –

  Poppy suddenly leans her head in her sister's lap.
    Beat.

Clover Lori used to make hideouts for us under the table.

Poppy Really?

Clover Yeah. With blankets and torches and everything.

  Silence. Suddenly sings:

  Come little leaves said the wind one day
  Come to the meadows with me and play
  Put on your dresses of red and gold
  Summer is gone and the days grow cold.

Poppy What?

Clover It's been going round and round in my head all day.

Poppy Sing it again.

Clover It's stupid.

Poppy But sing it.

Clover No. It's just a stupid nursery rhyme. I think we used to skip to it.
I don't know what it's doing in my head.

Poppy Did I used to skip to it, too?

Clover I don't know. I forget. And I forget how the rest of it goes.

Silence.

Poppy.

Poppy Yeah?

Clover Why do *you* think?

Poppy I don't know.

Clover Me neither.

Silence.

You know what Mum said, about Belfast.

Poppy Yeah.

Clover Well, I think that's a stupid thing to say.

Poppy Yeah.

Silence.

Clover 'Ring the bell and run away fast.'

Poppy What?

Clover Bell-fast.

Poppy Oh.

   Beat.

You got in so much trouble for that.

Clover Yeah.

   Silence.

Pops?
  In school and that – have things been – and don't tell
me things have been fine for you, because they certainly
haven't been fine for me.

Poppy (*reluctantly*) Yeah. Teachers keep keeping me
behind after class and asking if I'm okay.

Clover What do you say?

Poppy 'Yeah.'

Clover Me too.
  I hate it when they do that.
  Like they have any idea what it's like.
  Nosey fucking parkers.

Poppy (*giggling*) Clover.

   Silence.

Clover And, Poppy –
  Have any of those girls said anything lately?

Poppy No.

Clover Are you sure?

Poppy Yeah.

Clover You promise?

Poppy *Yes.*

Clover 'Cause, swear to God, Pops, if any of them says anything else /

Poppy It's okay, / Clover.

Clover No, Poppy, it's not okay – and I'm serious – if any of them says one word to you – stupid wee millies that they are – I'll kill them.

Poppy It's okay, Clover, you don't have to. I can look after myself.

Clover No, Poppy.
    'Cause I don't want people thinking *I'm* weird.
    'Cause see the thing is, Poppy, the thing is –
    You have to try to be as normal as possible.
    'Cause especially now, what with Lori and all that –
    People are going to be specially watching you to see if you're normal or not, too. And if anything happens, you have to tell me right away, okay? Not Dad and definitely not Mum and if I was you I wouldn't go telling the teachers, either. They'll just get involved and make things a hundred times worse. But you're to tell me if anyone says or does anything, okay? And you're to be as normal as possible.

    Beat.

Poppy I am normal.

Clover No you're not.
    Normal people don't sit under tables reading *Peter Pan*.

Poppy Leave me alone.
    You're just ragin' because when Lori's back you won't be the oldest any more.

Clover What?

Poppy You won't be the oldest any more and so / you won't be able to –

Clover shoves Poppy, hard. Poppy squeals.

Clover Shut up!
They treat us like children, Poppy, and it's your fault!
If you acted a bit less babyish /

Poppy / I do *not* act babyish!

Clover and a bit more grown-up then they'd treat us like
grown-ups for once!
Do you understand?

Poppy Leave me alone.

Clover No, Poppy!
This is serious!
I am serious!
Say you understand!
(*Shaking her.*) Poppy!
Say it!

Poppy Get off of me, Clover, get off, all right, I
understand!

Clover You understand?

Poppy *Yes!*

Clover Don't say it like that.

Poppy Please, Clovey! Stop it!

Clover No, Poppy. Somebody has to tell you.
Somebody in this family has to take charge of things.

Poppy Don't be silly.

Clover It's true and you know it.
Things are going to be weird when Lori's back. They're
going to be seriously weird –

Poppy / No they're not.

Clover – and you're a baby if you think they won't.

Silence.

Poppy Leave me alone, Clover.

Clover Fine. I'm going.
I was going anyway.

But she doesn't move.

SCENE FOUR

*It is four in the morning. David cannot sleep. He is
working on his book of place names at the living-room
table, dressed in his dressing gown. Phyllis enters, also
dressed in a dressing gown.*

Phyllis David. I woke up and you weren't there.

David looks up briefly and then returns to his books.

David Well, I couldn't sleep.
So I thought I may as well – (*Gestures at books.*)

Phyllis Yes.

*She hovers, pulls her dressing gown tighter around her.
Silence.*

Would you –
I mean a cup of tea or something, would you –

Beat.

D'ye know what I'd like, I'd like a hot whiskey. Would
you do me a hot whiskey?

David sighs.

David / Phyllis . . .

Phyllis Right.
Right.
Well d'ye mind if I –? (*Gestures at the sofa.*)

David shrugs.

David No, no, go on ahead.

Phyllis I was doing my head in, lying there not sleeping.

Silence.
Phyllis watches her husband. He does not look up.
After a while Phyllis clears her throat tentatively.

So what are you . . .
David?
What are you working on, then?

David coughs.

David Oh, you know, this and that. This and that.

Phyllis Anything . . . (interesting)?

David No, no, nothing exciting. Just – you know.
Checking a few things here and there. Making some
notes. That's all.

Phyllis Oh.

Silence. Suddenly; impulsively:

David.
Will you read to me, David?
Will you?
It doesn't matter if it doesn't make sense, I don't mind
that. Just –
Read to me, David?

Beat.

David 'C is eclipsed by g, as in *Cnoc-na-gceann*,
Knocknagin, the hill of the heads: a place of execution.
'*Ch* is a guttural sound which does not exist in English,
and in anglicised names it is often changed to an *f*, as in
Culdaff, *Cul-dabhach*: the back of the pool.'

Beat.

29

Phyllis (*she knows*) And what is –
   An eclipsis, again?
   Remind me?

David (*he knows she knows*) An eclipsis –
   An eclipsed consonant –
   Has its sound completely suppressed, the sound of
another consonant which is prefixed, being heard instead.

Phyllis Right. Of course.

David When *c*, for example, is eclipsed by *g*, it is written,
g-c, but the *g* alone is pronounced. In written English, the
eclipsed letter does not – exist, being always omitted.

   Beat.

Phyllis Read me the places themselves.

   Beat.

David Corlat, the round grey hill of the sepulchres.
   Corlea, grey round hill.
   Corlough, the lake of the *corrs* or herons.
   Cormeen, smooth round hill.
   Cornacreeve, the round hill of the branchy tree.
   Cornagee, Cornagheeha, the round hill of the wind.
   Cornahoe, the round hill of the cave.
   Cornamucklagh, the round hill of the piggeries.

   Beat.

Cornaveagh, the round hill of the ravens.
   Corratober, the round hill of the well.
   Corrinshigo, Corrinshigagh, the round hill of the ash
trees.
   Corrofin, the weir of Finna, a woman's name.
   Corskeagh, the round hill of the white thorns.

   Silence.
   Phyllis's eyes are closed. She sighs.

Silence.

Phyllis In a couple of weeks, perhaps, when things have
settled down.
We should take a trip up to Donegal, maybe.
For the day.
Or we could spend the night.

David Donegal.

Phyllis Drive down.
The two of us.
Clover and Poppy are old enough to look after
themselves for a night, and /

David *Dun-na-nGall*: the fortress of the *Galls*, or
foreigners.

Phyllis Lori will be here anyway, of course.

Beat.

David Long before the Anglo-Norman invasion, the
Danes founded a settlement there, hence its name in Irish.

Phyllis You need a break from it, David.
We need a break from – from it all.
It would be good to get away for a bit, you and me.
Get out of Belfast. Just for a night or so. You know?

David Belfast.

Phyllis We need to talk, David.

David *Beilfeirste*: the *bel* or ford of the *farset*, or
riverbank. /

Phyllis / David –

David A crossing point. The Irish *bel* does not signify
beauty.

Phyllis Come here to me, David.

We'll drive up.

I'll drive.

We'll leave early morning, and take sandwiches with us that we've made the night before.

We'll take tea in a flask, stop on the edge of the road, on the outskirts of Toome.

We'll cross over the Pass, and perhaps it will be misty, so that – so that we will feel as if we are flying, or as the road climbs higher, that we really are leaving the world behind.

David Right.

Phyllis Don't you think?

David Aye.

Phyllis What?

David Maybe.

Silence.

Phyllis David?

Are you going to tell me what Toome means now, is it?

Beat.

David 'Dolores'.

The name means 'sorrow'.

Why ever did we choose such a name, eh?

Phyllis Don't.

David We should have known better.

Phyllis Please, David.

David Tempting fate is what is was! Tempting / fate.

Phyllis Please!

David We should have known.

Phyllis A place or a person is more than a name.

David Aye, but names are powerful. Naming something creates a power over –

Phyllis As you know fine rightly, she was named after my grandmother /

David And I shouldn't ever have agreed to it.

Phyllis What?
Don't you dare!
Because names mean nothing!
Not in the way that you believe they do.
You can study places and names until the bloody cows come home but you're not going to find out what happened to her. And you're not the only one. You're acting as if you're the only one. You've got two other daughters. And me. What about me? Where do I fit in?

Beat.

I'm sorry.

Beat.

Oh Christ. I'm sorry, David.
I didn't mean –
I'm just –
Well all of us, aren't we, we're all just –

Silence.

I mean we're just nice, normal people, living in a nice, normal house. And she had a happy childhood. None of those English doctors or nurses is going to dare tell me she didn't! Whatever it was, it wasn't us! Because we did our best. We made sure we were out of the country over the Twelfth, we made sure they didn't see the worst of the news, we explained to them what was going on, and why it was wrong – didn't we? We kept the worst of it at bay

33

as best we could – sang songs when they couldn't sleep for the helicopters – we protected them from Belfast and encouraged them to set their sights beyond Belfast –

She stops abruptly.

Can you tell me, David, what we did or didn't do?

David We are where we come from, Phyllis, and there's no getting away from that.

Phyllis What?
What is that supposed to mean?
What do you mean by that?

David I just mean that you can't /

Phyllis 'We are where we come from'?
That's not true.
That's not true because if that's true there's no hope for any of us.

Silence.

David, will you talk to me, for Christ's sake?

David And where's talking going to get us?

Beat.

I came down to work.
Is there no peace to be had anywhere?

Silence.
Clover enters.

Clover.
What on earth are you doing out of your bed? It's four in the morning.

Clover (*sadly*) You can hear you upstairs.

David Go back to bed, Clover.

Clover I couldn't sleep, anyway.

Silence.

Can I . . .
Stay here with you for a bit.

Phyllis Oh Clover. This is ridiculous.
You heard your father. Away back to bed.

Clover 'Away back to bed, Clover' – Mum, you can't treat me like I'm a baby. Not now, not any more.

David Please, Clover.

Clover No, Dad!

Beat.

Phyllis (*gentler*) It's a school night, love.

Beat.

Clover That's what I – that's actually what I –

Beat.

Mum . . . (*In a rush.*) Mum, can Poppy and I have the day off school tomorrow.

Beat.

Phyllis No, you cannot.

Clover Oh but please, Mum? I've been thinking about it and I think /

Phyllis I said no, Clover. You have to go to school. And your sister's only just started secondary school, for Christ's sake. She can't start missing days.

Clover Well then, just me? Can *I* have the day off school?

David You heard your mother, Clover.

Clover But Dad /

Phyllis Please, Clover. Go to bed.

Clover But I want to be there. When Lori gets back. I want to be here when Lori gets back, oh please!

Phyllis You'll see her when you come home from school.

Clover But /

David No buts, Clover.

Clover Mum –

Phyllis Please, love, don't do this to me.

Clover But –

Phyllis Listen to me, Clover. I think it would be better – better for your sister – if it was just your father and I. We don't want to make a big deal out of it – (*To David.*) Do we. We think it's best – don't we – that things get back to normal as soon as possible.

Clover Yeah, but things aren't ever going to be the same, though, are they? Things are going to be /

Phyllis Don't do this to me, Clover – please – I'm warning you – please – just go to bed –

Clover Are you going to go to bed?

> *Beat.*

Phyllis Yes.
 Yes, of course. Shortly. Your father and I just have a few things that we need to . . .

> *Beat.*
> *Clover turns and leaves the room without a word.*
> *Silence.*

She's right, you know, we should –

> *Beat.*

36

Look, David. About tomorrow . . .

Beat.

About tomorrow, David.
    What do you think we should –
    I mean, after we've –
    Do you think we should –

Beat.

David (*without looking at her*) I've been meaning to say
to you, I think I'll –

Beat.

That is to say, after we've –

Beat.

I actually think I'll go into town, afterwards.

Beat.

Phyllis You –

David (*hurriedly*) I mean, yes, I'll be here in the morning,
of course, but I just thought –
    Well. What's the point in me hanging round here all
day. I mean, there's no need really, is there. Because as
you said, and you're right to say it, we want things to be
as . . . normal as possible, don't we. And so, I thought
I may as well use the opportunity /

Phyllis / Use the *opportunity*?

David – to go to the Linen Hall Library. On a weekday,
you know.
    It's always so crowded on Saturdays.

Beat.
    Phyllis tries to speak but cannot.
    David continues hurriedly without looking at her.

37

And I think I may have found an anomaly, here, you see. 'Cornamucklagh, the round hill of the piggeries.' *Muc*: 'pigs'. But *magh* means 'plain'. And the *Annals of the Four Masters* gives the name as Corna*magh*lagh, the round hill of the plains, which is . . .

He trails off.
Silence.

Phyllis (*standing*) Well, David, I –
I'm not sure what to say to you, I –

Beat.

If we'd been a churchgoing family –
I mean the way we, my brother and sister and I, were brought up –

Beat.

Never mind.
It's nothing.

Beat.

I'm going to bed.

Beat.
She pauses. She is waiting for him.
But David does not move, and he does not look up.
Phyllis turns and leaves abruptly.

SCENE FIVE

The following day.
Clover and Poppy have just come in from school. They are breathless and excited and buzzing with trepidation, jostling and interrupting each other.

Poppy Mum!

Clover Don't *shout*, Poppy.
  Mum!

  Phyllis enters. She has been crying and is trying to hide it.

Phyllis Girls /

Poppy / Is she back?

Clover / Did she get back okay?

Poppy Is she upstairs?

  Poppy makes to dash upstairs and Clover grabs her by the arm.

Clover Poppy –

Poppy Get *off*!

Clover Shut up –

Poppy Mum, tell Clover to get *off* of me –

Clover Would you shut up!
  / Mum is Lori back okay?

Poppy No *you* shut up –
  / Mum –

Phyllis Girls –
  Shh – calm down –

Clover But is she back?

Phyllis Your sister's upstairs, she was tired, she's gone to bed /

Poppy I'll go up and wake her / she'll want to see us –

Clover Would you let Mum speak!

Poppy Don't *talk* to me like that!

Clover Shut *up* for God's sake, Poppy –

Phyllis Clover –

Poppy Yeah, *you* shut up, Clover!

Phyllis You two, will you please just for one second, Christ –

Beat.

Clover Are you okay, Mum?

Phyllis I'm fine, Clover.

Clover Are you sure?

Phyllis I'm fine.

Clover But you look /

Poppy Leave Mum alone, Clover –
Mum, can we go up and see Lori now /

Phyllis Poppy, I think it's best if we leave your sister to rest.

Beat.

Poppy Oh.

Beat.

But why?

Clover Stupid –

Poppy Shut up –
Mum, did you hear that, Clover called me /

Phyllis Oh Poppy, please /

Poppy What, no, that is so unfair, I didn't do anything I /

Clover Give it a rest, Poppy –
Is she okay, Mum? Is Lori okay?
What – happened?

Phyllis Nothing – *happened*, we – your father and I, collected Lori from the clinic, and we came back here, and Lori was tired and went upstairs, and your father – and so your father – went on into town.

Poppy Dad went into *town*?

Phyllis To the Linen Hall Library.

Clover For his book.

Phyllis Yes.
For his book.

Silence.

Poppy And so then what?

Phyllis And then what?
And then nothing, your sister's been upstairs since.
Girls –
Look –
I'm going to have to ask you to be very grown-up /

Clover Mum.
Don't.
You don't need to –

Phyllis Yes, I know, but just let me say it, Clover –
It's going to be very hard on her, being back home.
Being back home like this. And I know it's going to be hard on the two of you, too – it's going to be hard on all of us. It's going to take a while –

Clover Yeah. We know. It's okay. We understand, Mum.
Don't we, Poppy.

Poppy What?
Yeah. Yeah, we understand.

Silence.

Phyllis She walked in through the front door and your father was getting the bags out of the car and she just turned and she had this funny smile on her face. And then she said, and it was the first time she'd spoken of her own accord the whole morning, and she said, this time three months ago she was getting ready to go to university, and here we were back where we'd started. I didn't know what to say and I asked if she wanted a hand unpacking her suitcases and she just – looked at me.

Beat.

Clover Yeah.

Beat.

Poppy Don't worry, Mum. Maybe she'll go back to university. After Christmas.
Do you think she will?

Phyllis I don't think so, Poppy. I doubt it.
Next year, perhaps, who knows.
Maybe Queen's, or, or Jordanstown. She can live at home, or if she wants to move out we can find her a flat nearby.

Beat.

But.
Let's not get ahead of ourselves.

Beat.

Clover, do you not have music practice on Fridays?

Beat.

Clover Yeah. It was cancelled.

Phyllis Was it now.

Poppy Yeah they –
Announced it in Assembly, Mum.

Clover Poppy.

And anyway, I didn't want anyone to ask me how the audition had gone. So.

Beat.

Poppy Did – did Lori see the card I made her?

Phyllis I left in on her pillow for her.

Poppy Did she open it?
I wrote a poem inside.

Clover You did what?

Phyllis I'm – sure she appreciated it.

Clover You wrote her a *poem*?
You just don't get it, do you, Pops /

Poppy Leave me alone.
Just cause *you* didn't do anything special.

Clover / Poppy

Phyllis / Girls . . .

Poppy (*sudden*) It's funny Lori being back.
The house feels different already.
Doesn't it?
You can tell it feels different.

Beat.

Clover Do you want a cup of tea, Mum?

Phyllis That'd be lovely.

Clover Right.
I'll – put the kettle on.
Poppy, will you help me?

Poppy Help you make a cup of *tea*?
Oh. Okay.

Clover You sit down, Mum. I'll bring it in here.

Phyllis does not move and Clover tries to manoeuvre her into a seat.

Go on, sit down, put your feet up.

Phyllis (*sharply, shaking herself free*) Clover, I appreciate this, but you don't need to – I mean I'm not –

Beat.

Clover (*brittle*) Right.
Come on, Pops.

Poppy Mum, Clover was only trying to / be nice –

Clover Leave it, Pops.
Come on.

The girls leave the room.

SCENE SIX

Later on: early evening.
Phyllis is sitting at the living-room table. There is a full pot of tea beside her but she hasn't poured it. She has a couple of brand new recipe books open in front of her – Gillian McKeith's You Are What You Eat Cookbook, How To Eat For Health And Happiness, The Optimum Nutrition Bible, *that sort of thing. But she is not reading them. She is lost in thought.*
Poppy sidles in. She is holding John Wyndham's The Chrysalids. *She hovers in the doorway – her mother doesn't look up – she slides into a seat beside her.*
Slight silence.

Poppy (Hi) Mum.

Phyllis Hello, love.

Beat.

Where's your sister?

44

Poppy Doing her homework.

Beat.

You mean –
   Lori's still in bed, I think.

Silence.

Dad's not back yet.

Phyllis No. No, your father's not back yet.

Beat.

Poppy Should I –
   Do you think she'd like a cup of tea or something?

Silence.

Mum?
   Do you think I should take her up –

Phyllis She'll come down when she's ready.

Poppy But do you think maybe someone should –

Phyllis I think we'd best leave her for the time being.

Poppy But –

Phyllis I don't know, love, I don't know.

Silence.

Poppy Shall I pour *you* a cup of tea?

She starts to pour. Then she stops.

This has gone cold. Shall I put the kettle on again?
   Mum?

Phyllis Oh, don't bother. I didn't really feel like tea anyhow.

Silence.

Poppy What are you reading? (*She reaches out and turns over the cookbook.*) Gillian McKeith? (*She giggles despite herself.*) Mum, why are you reading *You Are What You Eat*?

  Beat.

Phyllis I read somewhere – or perhaps I heard it on the radio – that –
  Well.
  Depression – that it can actually be caused by, by, a basic lack of B vitamins.

Poppy What?

Phyllis (*reads*) 'According to psychiatrists –' etcetera, etcetera . . . 'there are two kinds of depression, *exogenous*, which denotes depression resulting from outside factors,' and so on and so forth, here we are, '*endogenous*, which denotes a medical form of the illness resulting from internal biochemical sources.'
  (*As Poppy goes to speak.*) I know – but listen, 'Even marginal vitamin deficiencies can negatively affect your mood. Diets lacking in fresh natural foods and comprising low quality foods containing chemical additives, i.e. 'junk foods', can run down the system sufficiently to cause depression.'
  And I just wonder – you know, she was in halls, and probably not cooking properly, out – drinking, not taking care of herself – and I just –
  Well. I'm going to make sure that now she's back home, she eats – and all of us, for that matter – that she eats a healthy, balanced diet with plenty of –
  It can't hurt, that's all I'm saying.

Poppy Mum, it's not exactly as if we live on McDonald's or –

Phyllis Love –
  It can't hurt, is all I'm saying.

Beat.

Poppy Right.
So – what are you cooking tonight, then?

Phyllis Haricot bean and root vegetable stew with curly kale.

Beat.

Poppy Right.
Sounds –

Phyllis And *shiitake* mushrooms. The book says they're one of the most healing foods around. Here, you see– (*She finds the page and reads.*) '*Shiitake* mushrooms are a superb immune-system tonic.'

Beat.

Poppy Lori hates mushrooms.

Beat.

Phyllis Well, she's just going to have to get used to them then, isn't she.

Silence.

Poppy Mum, I wanted to ask you. What does 'abeyance' mean?

Phyllis 'Abeyance'?

Poppy It says that 'hostilities had been in a state of abeyance for several months and so a confrontation was inevitable and imminent'. It's in *The Chrysalids*. We have to do it for English.

Phyllis Have you looked up the dictionary?

Beat.

Poppy No.

Phyllis You should ask your father. He's the one who's good at words. But let me see now. It means 'inactive', I think. Or perhaps 'dormant' would be a better way of putting it.

Poppy Kind of like, things have been okay for a while but it hasn't gone away?

Phyllis More or less, I suppose.

Poppy Right.

   Beat.

Have you read it?

Phyllis *The Chrysalids*?
   Years ago.

Poppy It's a good book.
   I like it.
   And look. I got the one that used to be Lori's. When she did it in school. It was a boy in the other class had it. But I swapped him.
   Look.

   She shows Phyllis the inside cover of the book. Phyllis does not say anything.

Mum.
   Isn't that funny, Mum, that this was Lori's?

Phyllis Yes, love.

   Beat.

Poppy Mum, do you think it's true that that would happen?

Phyllis That what would happen?

Poppy All of –
   Well, I haven't got to the end yet so I don't know exactly how things are going to turn out. But I mean –

nuclear war and that – 'Tribulation', they call it – I know it's never going to happen to us. But *if* – like if there was a nuclear war or a terrorist bomb or something – do you think that'd be what it was like?

Phyllis Do I think *what* would be what it was like?

Poppy I don't know – I mean – like – everyone fighting each other?

Phyllis I don't think you need 'Tribulation' for everyone to fight each other.

Poppy No, but you know what I mean. And do you think – do you think that people would actually start to become psychic?
    'Cause I think –
    I mean, I know the other people, the ones that can't do the thought-pictures and that, I know they're scared of it – but I think –
    Just imagine –
    Imagine knowing *exactly* how someone else was feeling.

Silence.

Phyllis (*gently*) And don't you think, Poppy, that if we knew *exactly* how someone else was feeling, the, the – weight of it – we'd –
    Lose all capacity to carry on our normal, everyday lives?

Poppy What?

Beat.

I don't (know what you mean) . . .
    I just thought –
    You could tell someone exactly what you were feeling, or – like – show them how you were feeling. Wouldn't that be good? You'd be able to see exactly how happy or sad everyone else was. And so if they were feeling sad,

49

you'd know, and you'd be able to – I mean – you'd know
what to do, to make them better.

Silence.

Phyllis Poppy, love, it's a very sweet thought, but none of
us can know how Lori feels, or what she feels.

Beat.

Poppy I wasn't saying *Lori*, I was just saying –

Beat.

You're treating me like I'm stupid.
    Like I'm a little girl.
    I wasn't saying *Lori*.
    I only said it in the first place because we've to write an
essay on it, that's all. On 'Communication'. Except I just
wondered what you thought because I haven't finished
the book yet, and Clover says she's busy.

Phyllis When's the essay due in?

Beat.

Poppy Tomorrow.

Phyllis Had you better go upstairs and get on with it,
then?
    Oh, don't look at me like that, Poppy.

Poppy (*getting to her feet*) Well it's not my fault that I
haven't been able to finish reading it in this house, is it.

Phyllis Please, Poppy, not now.

Poppy 'Not now Poppy', 'not now Poppy' –

Phyllis You watch your tone of voice –

Poppy Why? Why should I? Why should *I* care what
you say? You don't care what *I* say. You just treat me like

I don't count. Or like I'm not even here. *I* hate mushrooms too, or had you forgotten? I hate them even more than Lori does, but it doesn't matter what *I* say, does it. Nobody cares what *I* think. I wish I lived in a *normal* family. As soon as I'm old enough I'm going to get out of here and I'm never coming back.

Phyllis You do that, Poppy.

Poppy (*thrown*) What?
  I mean it.

Phyllis So do I.
  You study hard and get out of here and never, ever come back.

Poppy What do you mean?

Phyllis I mean what I just said.

Poppy You're my *mother*, how can you even / say something like –

Phyllis I say it *because* I'm your mother, Poppy.
  You're right.
  Get out of here as soon as you can.
  Go as far as you can.
  And never come back.
  You don't want to live in Belfast.
  You don't want to bring up children in Belfast.
  In fact, you don't want to bring up children anywhere at all.
  Don't bother with children, Poppy. Whatever you do, you'll never manage to make things safe for them. One place is as fucked as another.

Poppy *Mum!*

  Silence.

Mum –

Beat.

You don't mean that.
   You don't mean that, Mum.
   Say it! Say you don't mean it.

   Beat.

Phyllis I'm sorry, pet.
   Oh, don't cry, now. I'm sorry.

Poppy You didn't mean it, did you?

   Beat.

Phyllis No.
   I didn't mean it. I didn't mean it.

Poppy Why did you say it if you didn't mean it?

Phyllis Love, I said I'm sorry.

Poppy But you shouldn't say things like that. You just
shouldn't say things like that.

Phyllis I won't say it again.

Poppy Promise?

Phyllis It was only words, Poppy.

Poppy *Promise.*

   Beat.

Phyllis Poppy . . .

   Beat.

All right then, I promise.

   Beat.

Now then.
   That's enough of that.
   Let me get dinner on.

Poppy Can I help?

Phyllis Thank you, love, but I'm fine.
  Are you going to get upstairs and finish reading that
book, then?
  Yes?
  That's a girl.

Poppy That's what Dad says.
  'That's a girl.'
  You don't say that. It sounds funny you saying that.

Phyllis 'That's a girl!'

Poppy (*tiny giggle*) Yeah.

Phyllis Okay then.

Poppy Okay.

  Beat.

I love you, Mum.

  Beat.

Phyllis I love you too, Poppy.

Poppy Okay.

  Poppy leaves the room.
    Phyllis watches her, and stands still for a moment.
    *Then she turns to the table and stares at the books
  for a second.*
    She closes the books and sits down.
    *Then she gets up again. She stands, staring straight
  ahead at nothing.*

I play Poppy

The Method of Physical Action = STAN.

SCENE SEVEN

That night.
  The table is set for five.
  Lori is not there.
  Nobody is really eating.
  Silence.

David This is ridiculous.

  Silence.

I won't be –
  Held hostage like this.
  Held hostage.
  Will one of you girls /

Clover She knows it's ready.
  Mum told her, didn't you, Mum.
  I'm not going to beg her to come down.

  Beat.

David Poppy, go and tell your sister one more time to
come down.

  Beat.

Poppy Mum?

  Beat.

Phyllis Do as your father says, Poppy.
  Beat.
    Poppy stands up.

Poppy What shall I say?

Phyllis Just say –

David Tell her we're waiting for her.

54

Clover But – (*She stops abruptly.*)

David What's that, Clover?

Clover No. Nothing.

David Away you go, Poppy.

> *Beat.*
>> *Poppy leaves.*
>> *Long silence.*
>> *Nobody meets anyone else's eye.*
>> *Poppy comes back in.*
>> *Beat.*

Poppy She says she's not hungry.

> *Beat.*

She says she's sleeping.

Phyllis (*to David*) She has had a long day.

David We've all had a long day.

Phyllis Sit down, Poppy.

> *Beat.*

I'll take some food up to her later.

David You will not. That's the worst possible thing you could do. The sooner things are back to normal the better.

Clover Dad's right, Mum.

> *Beat.*

(*Suddenly.*) Remember how you used to say that if we didn't eat our dinner you'd give it to us for breakfast, and if we didn't eat it at breakfast you'd put it in a Tupperware container and make us take it into school for break time?

She starts giggling.

Sorry, I –

Poppy Clover!

Clover carries on giggling uncontrollably.

Clover Sorry, I can't /
I can't help it, I –

Phyllis / Jesus wept.

David Get a grip, Clover.

Clover is inarticulate with giggles, almost crying.

Poppy Mum –
What's the matter with Clover –?
Clover!
Stop it, Clover!

Clover (*stopping giggling as suddenly as she started*)
I never saw how me eating my dinner would help the
starving babies.
   But of course me eating my dinner doesn't help them –
it's a question of –
   Respect –

She stands abruptly.

Clover I need a glass of water.

Phyllis Please, Clover –

Poppy Stay and finish your dinner.

Clover I need some fresh air.

She leaves.

Phyllis Is this how things are going to be?

Beat.

This can't go on.

Poppy Mum.

Phyllis I can't go on like this.

David It hasn't even started yet.

Phyllis I know. If this is the way things are going to be –
Is it too much to ask that a family sits down and eats together?
I'm asking you, is that too much to ask?

Silence.

Act Two

SCENE ONE

The garden.

That unreal time between night and the break of day in the early hours of the morning.

It is cold and dark and frosty, but still and windless; it feels as if the garden is somehow suspended outside of time. The branches of the apple tree are black and twisted and spindly, like charred limbs. There is no moon, or, if there is, it is hidden.

Lori is wandering, smoking.

A light goes on in a downstairs window, casting a muted pool of light over the lawn, which dissolves into the shadows.

If Lori notices the light, she does not react, or she does not care.

A moment later, Phyllis comes out of the house.

Phyllis You're smoking.
  I didn't know you smoked.

Beat.

Since when do you smoke?

Lori does not reply.

Well, it's your body.
  But I'm –

Beat.

Just don't do it in front of your sisters.
  They look up to you too much.

Lori No they don't.
  / Not any more.

Phyllis Oh, they do, you know.

Silence.

And the way they – rushed home from school to see you,
oh, they couldn't wait to see you. And you wouldn't even
so much as look at them.

Lori Mum – I couldn't.
How could I, Mum?

Beat.

Phyllis Well, you can't lie in bed all day. It isn't healthy.
You're not going to get better by lying in bed all day.

Silence.

What are you doing out here?

Lori Having a cigarette.

Phyllis I can see that.

Lori Well then.

Phyllis Lori –

She stops herself.
Beat.

Will you come inside? You'll catch your death.

Beat.

I didn't mean –

Silence.

Come on, pet. It's too cold to be outside.

Lori Then go in.

Phyllis Sorry?

Lori If you're cold, then / go in.

Phyllis Lori –

Lori I didn't ask you to come outside.
I'm not asking you to stay outside.
So go in. If you're cold then go in.
I'm not cold.

Phyllis Don't be silly, of course you're cold.

Lori I'm not cold.

Phyllis Of course you're cold.

Silence.

It's the middle of winter. It's freezing. Of course you're cold.

Lori Is that what you want, Mum, do you want me to agree with you, is it? If I say that I'm cold – and I'm not – but if I say that I am, will you leave me alone?

Beat.

Mum – please.
I just want to be alone.
Will you leave me alone?
Will you do that, Mum, will you leave me alone?

Phyllis I will do anything for you, Lori, anything.
But I'm not leaving you alone, not like this, not now.
All right? Do you hear me?

Silence.

Lori I shouldn't be here.

Beat.

Phyllis What?

Lori Here in *Belfast*, I mean.
Jesus.

Silence.

It's all wrong, me being back here.

Phyllis I know.

Lori Then why did you bring me back here? Why couldn't I, why couldn't I – I don't know – it's wrong, Mum – why couldn't I've stayed across the water?

Phyllis For goodness sake, Lori –

Lori No, I mean it, Mum, you shouldn't have brought me back here.

Phyllis And what were we supposed to do, eh, what were we supposed to do with you?

Lori What were you supposed to do with me?
    Jesus, Mum.

Phyllis I didn't mean it like that.

Lori What were you supposed to do with me?

Phyllis For crying out loud, will you stop twisting my words around.

  Beat.

I'm sorry.
    You're ill.
    You don't mean it.

Lori Oh, Jesus, Mum –
    Would you not –
    Oh, Jesus, would you not –

Phyllis Would I not? Would I not what?

  Beat.

Would I not what, Lori?

61

Lori Would you not –
Would you not –

Beat.

I just want to be alone, Mum.
Please.

Phyllis What can I do, Lori?

Lori Mum –

Phyllis What are we going to do?

Lori I –

Phyllis Can you tell me that?
What are we going to do?
Where do we go from here, and how? How do we –

Lori Mum, please, just leave it –

Phyllis Where did we go wrong, Lori? Was it something we did or didn't do? Because I've been trying and trying and I simply cannot understand –

Lori This isn't about you, Mum.

Phyllis What?

Lori I said / this isn't –

Phyllis I heard what you *said*, Lori –

Lori Well then.

Phyllis But I don't understand –

Lori It isn't about you, Mum. It isn't anything to do with you.

Phyllis Well, Lori, I don't know how you can say that because –

Lori You're embarrassed, aren't you, Mum.
See, you don't even try to deny it.

Phyllis Lori –

Lori Too late, Mum it's obvious, you're embarrassed of me. Oh I can just imagine it, your, your coffee mornings, or golf, or book club, or whatever – 'So how are your three, Phyllis?' 'Oh, my three are grand, well, two of them anyway, the other one tried to kill herself, bit embarrassing for all of us really' –

Phyllis You're ill, Lori. You don't know what you're saying. This isn't you talking.

Silence.

What happened to you, Lori?
    Did something bad happen to you over there?

Lori No, Mum – listen – you can't – there wasn't any – *one thing* –
    Mum.
    Look, Mum –
    I think – thinking about it – I think it's always been there, inside of me – the sadness – like a shadow – you know – and you can't – you can't – lose – your shadow you can't – trick it away from you, or – or snip it off and bundle it into a drawer, you know? It's not you, but it's part of you, and –
    Don't cry, Mum – Jesus –
    Mum, please –
    This is why, Mum –

As Phyllis goes to hug her:

Don't touch me, Mum – please – go away from me – this is why I can't – don't you see – this is why I can't –

Phyllis How did we fail you?
    We fed, and clothed, and loved you – Christ we loved you – *love* you – love all of you – we read (*past tense*) stories to you at night – took you to the playground and

63

pushed you on the swings – taught you to swim and to ride a bike – helped you with your homework, drove you to music lessons, to ice skating lessons, to your friends' houses – and these sound like little things but they aren't – we hoovered the monsters up from under the bed when you wouldn't believe that they were gone – do you remember that? – laughed when you laughed, cried when you cried – were happy so long as you were happy – were happy *whenever* you were happy. You were everything to us. We did everything it was in our power to do for you. We gave you everything it was in our power to give to you.

And I know that there have been times when – I mean not for one second am I saying that things have been in any way perfect, because of course there have been tears, and arguments, and –

But – Lori – can you tell me – please can you tell me –

Silence
  Lori does not say anything.
  Phyllis turns and walks away.

(*suddenly.*) well if you're not going to talk to me then let me tell you something, Lori.

When you were born – (*She chuckles despite herself.*) – there was a woman in the bed across from me who'd just had twins. I can't for the life of me remember her name, now. She was only a year or so older than I was, but they were her fourth and fifth, she had three others already, all under five I think – can you imagine! I didn't for the life of me know how I was going to manage with just the one. With you. I was terrified. I was too scared to pick you up in case I dropped you. And one night I told this to your woman. And the following day she hatched a grand plan – and I don't know how on earth she managed to persuade me to go along with it – but she did. She had lipstick and heated rollers in her overnight bag, and we dolled ourselves up, did our hair and what have you –

64

and then when the nurses took the babies away to bath them, didn't the two of us sneak out of the hospital and into the pub across the way. We had a Bloody Mary each, and your woman turns to me and says, you're going to be all right, so you are, your baby's not going to break.
'Your baby's not going to break.'

Now why I'm telling you this, Lori, why I'm telling this to you –

When we got back to the ward, visiting hour had begun, and your father was already there, and oh, he was furious with me for leaving you, absolutely furious. Anything could have happened, he said, anything – and I started crying, and – and I'm standing there, holding you, like this, just – looking at you, your fingers, and your toes, your eyelashes – everything about you, so – perfect, and I don't know what I've done to deserve you, and I don't know how I can ever, ever be – worthy of you. And all of a sudden I know that I would do anything for you. Anything. I will die for you, I will –

And that's something that never changes, something that never goes away, ever –

Because there's nothing that can break that bond, nothing, because – because I carried you inside of me, Lori, because – you were and are a part of me.

Beat.

Lori There's nothing that you can do, Mum.
Please, just – go. Just leave me alone.
There's nothing that you or anyone can do, or say, or, or be, that will make things all right again.
Just –

Beat.

Don't you see, Mum. Every single word you say makes things worse. Every word you say is another word that can't be – unsaid –

Look –

I can't bear to be near you, Mum. Do you hear me? I can't bear to see you, I have nothing to say to you, I just want to be alone. I'm asking you, will you please just – leave me be?

Long silence.
  Phyllis turns and walks a few steps away.
  Lori is motionless.
  After a while she lights another cigarette.
  Phyllis turns around and watches her.
  Lori does not look at her mother.

Phyllis Are you actually going to smoke another one?

Lori Dad smokes.

Phyllis Well, that's his business. Your father is an adult.

Beat.

Well, you're not to smoke in the house, understood? And I'd rather you didn't do it in front of me.

Lori (*suddenly stamping on her cigarette*) Fine. I'm going to go in now.

Phyllis What? But –

But Lori has left in the direction of the house.
  Phyllis stands for a second, and shivers.
  She bends and picks up the cigarette butts that Lori has left behind.
  She holds them clenched in her fist.
  She stands for a second, and then goes in.

SCENE TWO

Lori's room.
 Lori is sitting on her bed. The curtains are open.
 Poppy has just come in.

Poppy Lori.

 Beat.

You're awake?

 I heard voices. Outside. And it was you and Mum. And then I heard you coming up the stairs. So I waited for a bit and I didn't hear anything else but I just thought –

 I couldn't sleep either, Lori. And I know Mum said not to disturb you and if you want to rest I'll go away or if you want I can just sit here.

 Because I can't sleep either. I didn't want you to be on your own.

 And I wanted to give you this –

 I found it –

 It's a tape –

 Shall we play it? We can turn the volume right down so it doesn't wake anyone else up. Or if you like I'll just leave it here and you can play it in the morning but I thought –

 I mean, we don't have to but I just thought you might like to hear it because –

 Silence.

Lori What is it.

Poppy The tape?
 It's –
 Can I play it?

 Silence.

 Poppy goes to the CD player, kneels down and puts the tape in. She rewinds it.

67

Silence.
She presses play.

I think it's this side but it might be the other.

> *But the music starts: it is 'The Skaters' Waltz' from*
> *Emile Waldteufel's* Les Patineurs *(Opus 183).*
> *Poppy watches Lori.*
> *Lori does not cry.*
> *The two sisters listen in silence.*
> *The music finishes, and Poppy stops the tape.*

There!

> *Beat.*

Lori?
  Did you like it?
  It's 'The Skaters' Waltz'.
  You know?
  It always used to be your favourite, didn't it?
  Remember when you –
  Do you remember?

Lori (*slightly flatly*) God.
  The last time I –

Poppy Do you like it?
  Hearing it again, do you like hearing it?
  I thought you'd like it.
  I thought it would be – to hear it – a nice surprise?
  Was it, Lori? Was it a nice surprise?

> *Beat.*

Lori Yeah.

Poppy I missed you, Lori.
  I missed you a lot.
  And I'm glad you're back.
  I mean –

I'm not glad that –
But I'm glad you're back and things are going to be better now you're back.

Silence.

Can I – come and sit on your bed?

Beat.

Lori (*suddenly*) Is Clovey up?

Poppy What?
I – don't know.

Lori Will you see? Will you see if she's up, too?

Poppy Shall I wake her up, if she isn't?

Lori I don't know. No.
Yeah. Maybe.
Just – go and see, will you.

Beat.
Poppy turns and scampers out of the room.
Lori stays motionless.
Poppy and Clover come into the room and Poppy closes the door carefully behind them.
Beat.
Clover and Lori look at each other and Poppy looks from one to the other.

Poppy She wasn't awake but I woke her.

Silence.

Clover What did you want?

Beat.

Lori Nothing.
Just –
To see you.

Clover You had all day to see us.
I was asleep.

Beat.

Lori Go back to bed then.

Clover There's no point now.
I'm awake now.

Beat.

You had all day to see us if you wanted to.
We came home from school early.
I skipped music practice. I'm meant to have a solo in the Christmas concert. It's a big deal, Lori. And I lied to Mum about it and we came home early.
You had all day.
And Mum cooked dinner – a special dinner – special for you – and –

Lori I'm sorry.

Clover So you should be.

Poppy Clovey?

Clover (*without taking her eyes off Lori*) Yeah.

Poppy Please don't. We're here now. We're all here. It's all right now.

Clover So she thinks it's all right for her to spend all day in bed – not coming out, not speaking to anyone – and then to wake us up when we're trying to sleep?

Lori I'm sorry.

Clover That's not good enough.

Lori Then I'm sorry for that, too.

Silence. They stare at each other.

Clover So what did you want?

Silence.

Poppy She just wanted to see us, Clovey. She's been tired – haven't you, Lori? – it's not her fault – she's *ill* – she just wanted to see us. I think you're being –

Clover You think I'm being –?

Poppy Just stop it. Let's just be nice to each other.

Clover Right.
   Good plan.

Lori Please don't do this to me.

Clover Oh, I'm sorry.
   I forgot for a second that it was poor you.
   I forgot: you're the one that swallowed a whole bottle of fucking sleeping tablets and almost died and I forgot that we had to be nice to you because of it /

Poppy / *Clover!*

Clover You know what, Lori? You wouldn't've done what you did if you stopped to think for one second and remembered the rest of us.
   What do you think it's been like for us, then?

Poppy Shut up, Clover. Shut up, okay?

Lori I didn't mean it like that.

Poppy It's okay, Lori –

Clover You didn't mean what like what, you didn't mean the sleeping pills, was that a mistake, / because

Lori / I didn't mean –

Clover Do you know that you pretty much broke Mum's heart, for a start?
   Do you think there's a hope that she'll ever be happy again?

I always used to be so proud that you were my older sister. In school and that.

I mean, yeah, of course I hated it too, sometimes – I hated *you* sometimes – but most of the time I was so proud of you.

Lori You've grown up since I've been away.

Clover Yeah, you reckon?
Well you've –
You've –
(*Petulantly.*) Grown down.

Beat.
Clover, and then Lori, unexpectedly – despite themselves – and Clover very grudgingly – start to giggle. Poppy is bemused.

Stupid.

Poppy Stop it, you two – why are you laughing? What's so funny?

Lori Nothing.
Nothing's funny. Nothing at all.

Clover You have, though. You've got dead skinny. You look about twelve. You look like you should be the youngest out of all of us. Doesn't she, Poppy?

Lori I wish I could be twelve again.

Poppy It's not that great.

Clover You haven't even been twelve for the first time yet.

Poppy Shut up. I practically am.

Clover Lori – you'd hate to be twelve again, anyway.
I know I would. Remember how shit being twelve actually is.

Poppy (*hotly*) Yeah, especially if you've got older sisters who treat you like –

Clover Shush, you'll wake Mum and Dad.

Beat.

And don't be silly, Lori. 'I wanna be twelve again', it's not as if your life's over.

Poppy Clover!

Clover Don't you be telling me what I can and cannot say, Poppy.

Silence.

Lori C'mere, Pops. Come and sit here.

Beat.

Poppy Come on, Clovey. Let's just be friends.

Clover There's not room for three.

Poppy Yes there is!

Clover I'm not – *cuddling up* on Lori's bed, okay?

Poppy You're horrible, Clover. You always have to spoil everything.

Clover Piss off, Poppy.

Poppy Shut up!

Clover Shut up? Shut up? No, I will not shut up!
     'Cause, Poppy, I want Lori to answer my questions! Like why did she stay hidden away in her room all day? Does she have any idea how horrible it was at dinner time? Does she have any idea how horrible it's been?

Beat.

Poppy She's. Ill. Clover.
     Ignore her, Lori.

73

Silence.

Clover Well, if you've got nothing to say for yourself then –

I'm going back to bed.

Poppy Go on, then.

We're fine just the two of us, aren't we, Lori.

Clover I mean it. Unless you – unless you have anything to say, I'm going back to bed right now.

Lori Clovey, in the –

Beat.

When I was in the clinic – on the ward – I couldn't sleep – the sound of other people, you know, their breathing, and, and the little whimpering noises they'd make in their sleep. For the first couple of days they gave me pills, you know, and you'd just pass out and be unconscious till the morning. And then the last two nights they didn't, and I lay there trying to think myself somewhere else. And I thought – do you know what I thought of – do you remember when we used to play Bedknobs and Broomsticks on the bed in the spare room?

Clover So?

I don't see what that has to do with anything, Lori.

Lori Well –

Where would you go, if you could go anywhere?

Clover What?

I don't know.

Anywhere?

Lori Yeah, like it can be anywhere, like from when we were little or anything. It doesn't even have to be real.

Clover I don't know –

Lori Anywhere . . .

Clover I don't know.

Lori Where I decided on, was Donaghadee.
 The lighthouse at Donaghadee.

Clover Right.
 But – Lori – I don't know what you're saying.

Lori Remember every time Dad test drove a new car
we'd all pile in and drive up to Donaghadee?

Clover (*despite herself*) The way the cars always smelt.

Lori And we'd always get an ice cream –

Clover (*despite herself*) Oh yeah, from the Italian place.
 And you always got Pooh Bear.

Poppy I don't remember that.

Lori Oh, you were probably too young – this is, like,
when me and Clovey were wee, isn't it, Clovey –

Clover Yeah, 'cause it was before Grandpa died, wasn't it,
'cause after he died Dad would never go to Donaghadee
any more.

 Beat.

Lori That's right. But do you know why it's the place
I chose? 'Cause when we were driving back, over
Craigantlet, and you could see all of Belfast, and the
lights were just beginning to come on –
 Mum said, once, that when we were really little, we
used to think all the lights were fairyland. I like that. I
mean I can't remember it – I've tried and tried and I can't
actually remember it at all, but I like it that we thought
that.

 Beat.

Do you understand what I'm trying to say?

Beat.

Clover No, Lori – no – actually – I don't.

Lori I don't know how to say it any other way.
You really don't understand?

Beat.

You remember, though?

Clover Yeah but Lori what's *remembering* got to do
with –

Poppy *I* remember.
Fairyland. I remember that.

Beat.

Lori You don't remember that, Pops.

Poppy I do!

Lori You don't. There's no way you can remember that.
You weren't born yet.

Poppy I want to remember what you two remember.

Lori But you weren't there, Pops! Or else you were too
young to –

Poppy That's what you always say.
You always say, / 'You're too young, Poppy –'

Clover Poppy . . .

Poppy No, it's not fair!
All my life, Lori, all my life you've always said, 'You're
too young, Poppy.'
Like when the two of youse used to play Stick in the
Mud with – (*Flaps her hands as she gets increasingly
flustered.*) – with that boy and girl who used to live next
door but one –

76

Clover Pops –

Poppy *No*, Clovey, I want to say this – when you two used to play and, Lori, you never used to let me play.

Clover Poppy –

Lori You were too little, Poppy. Your legs were too short.

Poppy That!
That's what you always said!
'You're too little, / Poppy, your legs –'

Clover You used to cry when you were It.

Poppy What?

Clover You used to cry / when you –

Poppy Only because I could never run fast enough to catch you.

Lori Exactly, Pops, see, it wasn't your fault, you were just too little to –

Poppy But, Lori, I've always been too little.
I used to think that when I got to your age – whatever age you were – or Clovey's age –
But by then you were always bigger.
And by the time I was old enough to play Stick in the Mud properly you never wanted to play any more because you were all into – make-up, and boys.
If I had sisters, Lori, that were the age of Clover and me when you were my age –
I'd love them.
I'd play with them all day. I'd never be too bored or too grown-up to play with them. And I would never, *ever* laugh at them, or run so fast they couldn't keep up, or –

Lori Well, good for you, Poppy.

77

Poppy What?

Lori I said, good for you.

You'd make a much better sister than I ever was.

I'm a failure even at being a sister, I know, I don't need you to tell me.

So – good for you.

Beat.

Clover There's no need for that.

There's no need to be –

Poppy You're not a failure, Lori, don't say that.

Beat.

Mum found one of your old school photos the other day – it was of your ballet class. And she thought it was me and I was like – Mum – since when have I done ballet? And I looked so like you Mum left it out for Dad to see. And when Dad came home, he picked it up and said, Poppy, since when have you done ballet? But it was you.

Lori You're not me, Poppy.

Beat.

Poppy What?

Lori I said you're not me.

Poppy I heard what you said –

Lori Well then.

Poppy I wasn't saying that I was.

I was just saying –

I was just trying to be –

Clover Leave her alone, Lori.

Lori What?

Clover Picking on Poppy, it's pathetic, you're almost twenty she's not even twelve. Leave her alone.

Poppy I don't need you to stick up for me, Clover.

Lori (*to Clover*) Since when did you become the chairman of us?

Clover (*at Lori*) You're stupid if you want to be like her anyway, Poppy.
You're better than her. We both are.

Poppy Shut up, Clover.

Beat.

Clover I'm going back to bed.

Beat.

You should go back to bed too, Poppy.

Beat.
Poppy does not move.
Clover turns and leaves.
Silence.

Lori You should go to bed too, Poppy.

Poppy What?
Why?

Lori It's – late.

Poppy I don't mind! I don't mind that, Lori!
Shall I play the tape again?
'The Skaters' Waltz'? Shall I play it?

Lori No.
No. Not – now.
You should go back to bed.

Poppy Lori can I –
Can I stay with you?

Can I sleep in your bed? I won't take up much room, and I won't kick or anything –

Lori I don't –

Poppy Please, Lori?
I don't think you should be –
I just want to, is all.
Please, Lori?

Lori I think you should go back to bed.

Beat.

Poppy (*crestfallen*) Fine.
All right, Lori.

She gets up and goes to the door. She lingers in the doorway.
Beat.

Lori Go to bed, Poppy.

Poppy I just wanted to say, Lori –
I'm glad you're back.
I was the one that made the card, and – and wrapped the presents, and everything.

Lori Right.

Poppy waits for a second, but Lori doesn't say anything, and Poppy leaves quickly.
Lori stands in the middle of the room.
She goes over to the wall and gazes at the photo collage.
She pulls down one of the photos and stares at it.
She lets it drop to the floor.
She pulls down another; drops it. And another.

The following day.
  David is working on his book of Irish place names.
  Lori comes into the room.
  He looks up and attempts a smile.

David How are you feeling?

Lori (*shrugs*) Yeah.

David Good, that's –

  Silence.

Lori (*for something to say*) So –
  Where's Mum.

David I –
  Is she in the kitchen, maybe.

Lori Oh.
  Maybe.

  Beat.

And where are, uh –
  Pops and Clovey?

David Clover has music practice on Saturday mornings,
doesn't she.

Lori Oh.

David And I think Poppy has gone round to a friend's
house.

Lori Right.
  Dad –

  Beat.

David Yes?

Lori Nothing.

Beat.

David If you're hungry, I think there's some of last night's dinner in the fridge.
Your mother made –
'Haricot bean and root vegetable stew with curly kale.'

Lori Right.
I'm not really hungry.

David No.

Beat.

Lori I just couldn't – yesterday I mean – I just couldn't –

Beat.

David Right.

Lori And I'm sorry it's just –

Silence.

David You should eat something now, though.
Get your strength up. You can't expect to feel better if –

Lori Yeah, I'm just not –

David Right.
You should try to eat something, though.

Lori Yeah. I know.

Silence.

David Yes, well.

Beat.

It's good you're up.
Feeling better.

Silence.

Well.

*He coughs awkwardly, and then smiles and looks
away.*
  He returns to his notes.
  Lori stands watching him.

Lori Is that your book, Dad?

David My what.
  Yes, yes, it is.

Lori Right.

  Beat.

What are you –
  I mean, anything –

David Oh, this is just a –
  This bit's necessary, but not particularly interesting.
  I'm –
  I'm cross-referencing a couple of place names in the
Annals, that's all.

Lori Oh.

David Nothing exciting, I'm afraid.

Lori Right.

  Silence.

You've hardly spoken to me since I got back, Dad.

  Beat.

Dad.

  Silence.

David I don't know what to say to you, Lori.
  I don't know what to say to you.

Lori You don't have to *say* anything, I don't want you to
say anything, I just want you to –

David (*slowly, not looking at her*) You've crossed a line, Lori.

    I'm afraid you've –

    Beat.

And you have to understand, it's going to take time.

    It's about – trust. Because how do we know we're not going to walk in on you –

    Beat.

I'm sorry.

    Look, Lori –

    Beat.

I'm afraid I can't have this conversation with you.

    Not now. Not yet.

    Silence.
       Then Phyllis enters.
       She looks from her husband to her daughter.
       Beat.
       Then she speaks.

Phyllis You're up, Lori.

    That's great.

    How are you feeling?

Lori Mum –

    Beat.

Phyllis You should get dressed.

    No point sitting around in your pyjamas all day, is there now.

David Leave her be, Phyllis.

Phyllis What's that?

David Just –

84

Phyllis (*brittle*) Oh, I'm sorry, David.
I'm only her mother, after all.

Lori Don't, Mum.

Phyllis What's that, Lori?

David Look, Lori and I were just –

Phyllis Oh, I'm interrupting, am I?

David We were just having a little chat, that's all.

Phyllis Well.
Well, then I shall leave you to it.

Lori Mum –

Phyllis Don't worry, I can tell when I'm not wanted.

Phyllis turns quickly and leaves.
Silence.
The front door slams.
Silence.

Lori I don't know what to do, Dad.
I don't know what to do to make things okay again.

Silence.

Say something.

Beat.

Please, Dad –

David Give it time, Lori.
Your mother's –
Your mother's been –
Just give it time.
I don't know what else to say to you.

Silence.

Lori Is that it, Dad?
  Is that all –

David Just tell me what you want me to say, Lori, and
I'll say it.
  Just –
  Say the word, and I'll –

  Beat.
    He cannot finish the sentence.
    Silence.

Lori I need some boxes.

David Sorry?

Lori Boxes, cardboard boxes, I need some –

David Right.
  There are some in the, in the garage, I think.

Lori Right.

  Silence.

Right.

  Beat.

Like, like packing boxes.

David Packing boxes, yes.

Lori Right.

  Silence.
    David does not look at his daughter.
    Lori turns and leaves.

Late afternoon.
  Lori's room.
  Lori is kneeling on the floor, sorting out books etc. into
cardboard boxes. There is a small pile of things, and on
top of the pile is the tape of 'The Skaters' Waltz'.
  Clover enters, subdued and tentative.

Clover Lori?
  Can I come in?

  Silence.
    Clover looks round the room.

Your room looks really different now. Bigger. Or maybe
smaller. I can't tell.

  Lori shrugs.

Do you need a hand or something.

Lori No. I'm just . . .

Clover Oh.

  Silence.

Are you okay.

Lori What?

  Silence.

Clover Here, Lori.
  There're some really nice flats near Carrickfergus,
Mum was saying about them. New ones. Right beside
the water. You can see the castle from them. And they'd
be handy for Jordanstown, if you wanted to go to
Jordanstown. And I'd come and visit, I'd come and visit
you every day, if you wanted me to.
  Lori?

87

Lori Yeah.

Clover Do you think that's a good idea, Lori?

Beat.

Lori Yeah.

Beat.

I'm not going to go to Jordanstown, Clovey.

Clover Oh.
Oh.

Beat.

But maybe you should think about it, anyway.

Lori Yeah.

Silence.

Look, Clovey . . .

Clover (*hopefully*) Yeah?

Lori Nothing.

Silence.

Poppy found the original tape of 'The Skaters' Waltz'.
Do you want it?

Clover What?

Lori 'The Skaters' Waltz', do you want it?

Clover What?

Lori It's on that pile there.
And there's some – books and stuff. Couple of photos.

Clover Don't you want it?

Beat.

Lori If you don't want it, fair enough.

Clover But Lori –
    You can't just –
    Decide –
    That you don't want 'The Skaters' Waltz' any more.

Lori shrugs.

Lori There's so much stuff, Clovey.

Silence.

Clover (*picking up the tape*) Is this it?

Lori Yeah.

Clover If you don't want it, then I don't want it either.

Lori Fair enough.

Clover I'm serious, Lori.

Lori Yeah.

Clover No, but I'm serious.

Beat.
    Clover gets to her feet.

Lori?

Lori does not say anything and does not look up.

Lori?
    This is what I think of the stupid tape, Lori – this is
what I think of –

*She is crying. She rips the reel of tape from inside the
cassette. Then she stops.*

Look what you've made me do.
    It's ruined now. It's ruined.

Lori Clovey?

Clover runs out of the room.
    Silence.

89

Lori scoops up the tape and drops it into a box.
Poppy enters.

Poppy Are you okay, Lori?
I heard the shouting.
Was Clover being nasty to you?
Do you want me to tell her to leave you alone?

Lori It's fine, Poppy.
Look, I've got stuff to do.

Poppy Oh.
Are you tidying your room? Mum keeps saying I should
tidy mine, too. Do you want me to help you?

Lori No, Poppy. I need to be alone.

Poppy Oh.
Do you want me to keep you company? I could just sit
here and read or something.

Lori No, Poppy.

Poppy Oh.
(*Sadly.*) Clover was always your favourite, wasn't she.

Lori What?

Poppy You always liked Clover best. Out of me and
Clover. You always liked her best.

Lori That isn't true.

Poppy I know it is.
You have jokes that only the two of you get.
You have memories that only the two of you remember.
Even when Clover's being horrible to you you still like
her better.
I'm not stupid you know.
There's nothing that's just me and you, is there.

Beat.

Lori I remember –

Do you know what I remember.
I remember –
When you were born.

Poppy What?
Really?

Lori Yeah yeah, I do.
It's one of my first proper memories.

Poppy Don't be silly. You were eight when I was born.
You have loads of memories before me.

Lori No, but do you know what I remember.
I remember, I remember how cold it was the night you were born, the coldest night of the year, probably, and outside everyone's breath was like clouds of little stars.
I remember in the Ulster, standing on my tiptoes to look into the, the plastic cot where you were sleeping. And Mum had bought me and Clovey these dolls, they were the sort that said Mama and their eyes opened and everything, and I didn't want mine, I just wanted to look at you, your wee screwed-up face.

Silence.

Poppy Really?

Lori Yeah.
And then the nurse comes and says that Mummy needs to rest now, come along there's a good girl, and I'm clinging to the cot because I don't want to leave, there now don't be bold you're not going to be a bad, bold girl are you now, and I start crying, come along, you'll see your mummy tomorrow sure – and I say, I say, and I remember saying this, I say, but it's my *sister* I don't want to leave. I loved you so much, Poppy, right away I loved you so much, I loved you more than anyone.

Silence.

Poppy (*quietly*) I know it's not true.

91

Lori What?

Poppy It's a nice story but I know it's not true.

Lori What do you mean?

Poppy I was born in the Royal, not in the Ulster.
  It was – Clover was born in the Ulster.

Lori What? We were all born in the Ulster.

Poppy No. You and Clover. I was born in the Royal.

Lori Well – Royal, Ulster, what does it matter if I get the
name of the place wrong? God, Pops – the rest of it's true.

Poppy Is it?

Lori Of course.

  Beat.

And do you know what, you were born after the
Ceasefire, Poppy, and because of that I think there's
hope for you. I don't know if that makes any sense to
you, but I think you should remember it because you
might need it some day.

  Beat.

Poppy But Lori?

Lori Jesus Christ, Poppy. Just leave it, please?

  Beat.

Now please, Pops. There's stuff I need to do.
  Go find Clovey or something.

Poppy Okay.
  Okay, Lori.

  Poppy stands for a second, then runs out of the room.
  Beat.
  Lori curls up on her bed.

The living room.
  David reading.
  Phyllis enters. She is wearing an outdoor coat and
slippers.
  David looks up at her.
  Silence.

David Where did you go?

Phyllis Nowhere.

  Beat.

Tesco's car park. I sat there for over an hour. I couldn't
get out of the car because I was still wearing my slippers.

  David chuckles despite himself. Phyllis laughs
  reluctantly as well.
    They stop laughing.
    Slight silence.

Oh David.

David It's all right.

Phyllis I'm sorry.

David It's all right, Phyllis.

Phyllis I shouldn't have – stormed out like that.
  It was wrong of me.
  We have to stick together.
  All of us.
  We're a – *family.*

David Yes.

  Beat.

93

Phyllis I always used to think we were such a good family, you know? I mean as families go –
  And now look at us, you know?

David I know.

  Silence.

Phyllis Well.
  Has Lori been down again?

  Beat.

David No.

Phyllis Right.
  I'll go up in a bit then. Check on her – /

David / Phyllis . . .

Phyllis See if I can persuade her to eat with us.

David Yes.

Phyllis Do you think she will?

David I don't know.

Phyllis No.

  Beat.

Well.

  Silence. For something to say:

And where are the girls?

David Upstairs, I think. It's been quiet. I think hostilities are temporarily in abeyance.

Phyllis (*faint laugh*) Poppy.

David Aye.

Phyllis I hope you didn't write the entire bloody thing for her.

Pause.

They'd been getting on so well, hadn't they.
    And now the way they're at each other like cat and dog.

David (*slowly*) It's funny, isn't it, out of all of us, I think Clover's taken it hardest, in many ways.

Phyllis What makes you say that?

David Whenever you think of them – when they were younger – I've been thinking about it – it's always Clover running after Lori, doing what Lori does, going where Lori goes, wanting what Lori wants. And now – /

Phyllis / David –

David Please – listen to me –
    And now, Lori's been to a place where none of us can follow. A place where none of us can reach her –

Phyllis She's upstairs, David.

David No, Phyllis –
    When I went over to England, to collect her from the hospital –
    She didn't seem to know or maybe it was she didn't care what was going on any more. And I – hugged her, I just – what else could I do, I just hugged her, and I picked her up and carried her to the car, and – and I strapped her in, and –
    And driving back all through England, and Scotland, and then the ferry –
    And neither of us saying anything because – because – there is nothing to say –
    And such – peace, the whole time, so – peaceful –
    And it was as if – as if –
    In that moment, Phyllis, *in that moment* –
    I was closer to her than ever, and because we'd been so close –

We were closer than we'd ever be again. Than we ever could be again. As if that was the price to pay.

And that was when, Phyllis –

That was when I realised –

Silence.

Phyllis David . . .

Silence.

David Will you – (*He breaks off.*)

Can you – (*He breaks off again.*)

They stare at each other.
Neither of them moves.
Neither of them speaks.
Silence.
Clover and Poppy trail into the room.
Beat.

Poppy Can we come and sit in here with you or are you working, Dad?

Beat.

David You can, of course you can, it's the living room.

Beat.

Phyllis I'm going to get dinner on.

Beat.
David says nothing.
Phyllis turns quickly and leaves.

Clover (*flatly*) Is Mum okay.

David sighs.

David She's –

Silence.

How are you girls?

Poppy looks at Clover. Clover shrugs, then walks over to the sofa and curls up, tucking her feet underneath her. Poppy cuddles up beside her.
    Silence.

Poppy I thought Lori being back would make things okay again. I really thought it would.

Silence.

Mum spoke to Lori the night before – the night before she –
    And she said that afterwards she went over and over the conversation in her head, trying to look for clues. But she said Lori just seemed – normal. There's no way of knowing what's actually going on in someone's head. We could all be sitting down at dinner and – it could just seem normal, but it wouldn't be, and none of us would know until afterwards, and even afterwards we wouldn't understand. And you can go over and over and over things in your head and still not know how to understand them.

Beat.

David Poppy . . .

David stands up.

C'mere, Poppy.

Beat.
    Poppy gets up slowly and shuffles over to her father. He hugs her.

We'll make everything okay, Poppy. We'll try our best to –
    I promise you –
    And you too, Clover –
    I promise that we'll try our best to –
    And it isn't always easy.
    But we'll try our best –
    All of us –

97

Poppy How can anything ever be okay, Dad?

David It will be, Poppy.
  We'll make everything okay.
  Do you hear me, Clover?

Poppy Clover, come here.

  Beat.

Clover (No) Poppy . . .

David Clover, love, don't –

Clover Don't what, Dad?

David Don't –
  Don't be so hard on yourself.

  Beat.

Now, girls, shall we –
  Shall we light a fire in here then, eh?

Poppy You can't light fires, Dad.
  The ozone layer.

David Well, just this once shall we?
  The first and only fire of the year.

Clover Yeah, let's, Dad.
  I'll give you a hand.

Poppy Okay, I will too.

David That's my girls.

SCENE SIX

Lori's room. Lori is sitting on her bed.
  *The room is bare now. No photographs or posters on
the walls. Everything packed up in boxes. The boxes
piled up.*

Phyllis is taken aback, but tries to hide it.

Phyllis Goodness me.
   Haven't you been busy.

   Lori says nothing.

Did you –
   Did you fancy a – new start, is that what it is.
   It's a – good idea.
   We can – why not – redecorate the whole room, if you
like.
   There's a new Habitat opened in the city centre, they
have some nice . . .

   Phyllis turns away.
      Silence.

Lori Mum?

   *Phyllis turns back quickly and sits down on the edge
   of the bed.*
      She smooths Lori's hair. Lori does not react.

Phyllis Yes, sweetheart?

Lori Did you hear the helicopter last night?

Phyllis What?
   I don't – I don't think so.
   Perhaps I didn't notice it?

Lori I always think, you know –
   When you see pictures of –
   Of –
   Of – I don't know – of Iraq, or Kabul, or wherever –
   Places where there is real fighting going on –
   Helicopters overhead – that sort of thing –
   And remember the times when we were little and we
couldn't sleep because of the helicopters?
   And I think of –

99

I wonder if there are – and I mean there must be – other little children who can't sleep, and I wonder if their mothers are telling them to – ignore the sound, or to pretend it isn't there, like you used to do, so that they can get to sleep.

And when I think about it, the thing is that I can't sleep, either.

You know?

Phyllis (*carefully*) I think – I think, perhaps, that you should try not to think about – about –

I think that you should just try and concentrate on getting well again –

Lori But Mum –

How can you not think about it?

And I don't mean – *you* – I mean – anyone –

Once you've thought about it – once you've realised –

How can anyone – *not* think about it?

Phyllis I don't know what to say, Lori.

Silence.

Lori Mum?

Phyllis / Yes, sweetheart –

Lori Mum, do you think things get better?

Phyllis (*quickly*) Of course they will, sweetheart, of course things are going to get better, you're going to be absolutely fine and –

Lori I don't mean that, I don't mean me. I mean – things. Do you think that things – life – people – ever get better?

Beat.

Phyllis Of course they do.

Lori Because I don't think they do. I'd like to think that –

I'd like to be able to believe that things get better and people get happier but I don't think that's true.

Phyllis / Lori, sweetheart –

Lori I think – I think that things go on the way they always have been. I think that we think things change – or maybe we just have to believe they do – or pretend – I think that – yeah, sometimes people are happy – or think that they're happy – but I don't think they get happier. I don't think that things ever really get any better.

Phyllis Things are better for you than they were for me, Lori. My father used to beat my sister and brother and I. For no reason at all. He wasn't a bad man – he was a strict man, but he wasn't a bad man – that was just the way things were, then. One Sunday, when I was nineteen – your age – he caught me wearing lipstick and he trailed me into the bathroom and made me scrub my face and said I was no better than a whore, and he hit my mother when she tried to intervene.

Things have got better.

Lori Why, because I can wear lipstick? Because Dad doesn't hit us? That – Mum – that doesn't mean anything to me. I'm sorry – I'm sorry for you that things were tough – but that doesn't make me any happier.

Phyllis You are much happier than I was and don't you dare say that you aren't.

Lori says nothing.

Do you hear me?

Lori says nothing.
Beat.

I'm sorry.

Lori No – I'm sorry, Mum.

Phyllis Just –
  Hearing you talk like this, Lori –
  It's –
  It's not – *you*. It's not –
  I mean, I don't understand –
  Can you try and explain it to me, explain to me how
you feel, or, or why, because –

Lori There's nothing else I can say, Mum. I can't say it so
as you'll understand.

Phyllis Try me, Lori – please – just – give me a chance –
  Please, sweetheart –

  Beat.

Lori (*carefully*) Mum – when I think of – of my
grandparents, and their grandparents, and their
grandparents, and back and back and back – and what,
really, did they live and die and struggle and fight for?
For the hope that things would get better? For the (*quote
unquote*) 'generations yet unborn'? For *me*? Because –
because – in that case – if that's the case – then their lives,
their deaths, everything – it was pointless. It was pointless,
all of it, just – pointless.

  Beat.

You see, Mum, there's nothing you can say.

Phyllis You're ill, Lori. You're not thinking clearly.

Lori No, but Mum –

  Beat.

Once you've realised that – you can't go back to the way
things were, because –
  Mum, please –
  Don't cry, Mum, please –
  Mum –

You need to listen, Mum, because I need you to know this –

I want to go back, I'd give anything – I want to believe in things the way I used to believe in them, the way I used to believe in them without even thinking about it – without even knowing that I *was* believing. But I can't, Mum, I can't – and it isn't even that it's I don't know *how* to, it's that I know I can't – and so I can't see how I can go on – go on – living – because – because –

I don't think there's any such thing as the future, Mum. I think that life is just made up of moments, and outside each moment there's nothing else, and we have to believe that we're living in something bigger, something more coherent, because otherwise – otherwise we'd give up. I think that people need to believe that things get better – that one day, life on earth will be – beautiful – or else what would be the point of anything? It's like – it's like if you don't believe in Heaven then you have to believe in Earth – or you have to believe that Heaven is a place that you can find – or create – or whatever – on Earth, but – and the only way I can say this, and you're not going to understand me, anyway, but the only way I can put it is that I don't believe in Earth, either.

Phyllis What about us, Lori?

What about your dad and I? What about your sisters?

Lori I'm sorry, Mum.

Phyllis Do you think there haven't been times when I've wanted to leave you? To leave all of you? Do you think there haven't been times when I've wanted to – to – to do the things you do, to – travel, to go to university, to even *have* the possibility that you can go anywhere and do anything you like? I don't live *through* you and your sisters, Lori, I live *for* you. And that's why you – that's why one – 'goes on'. That's why you 'believe'. You go on – even when you think that you can't go on, or when you can't see how you can go on – you go on because there are other people – because other people depend on you – because other people are a part of you, too.

Silence.

Lori?
   Do you understand?
   Do you understand what I'm telling you?

Beat.

You're nineteen, Lori, and you've got your whole life ahead of you.

Silence.

Lori I'm sorry, Mum.

Silence.
   Phyllis closes her eyes and hugs Lori tight to her.
   At first Lori does not move.
   Then she closes her eyes and clings to her mother.
   Silence.
   Lori is the first to break the embrace. And she seems somehow brighter – stronger – resolute.

Phyllis I came up to tell you that dinner's ready.

Lori Right.

Phyllis Will you please come down, Lori?

Beat.

Lori Yes.
   All right.

Phyllis You will, you'll come down and eat with us?

Lori Yeah. I will, yeah.

Beat.

Phyllis Right.
  Well, Lori –
  That's –
  Great, that's – great.
  (*Fiercely.*) We're going to beat this together, Lori. We will. We'll beat this together.

Lori Mum –

  Beat.

Listen, Mum.
  You go on down, okay?
  I'll –
  I mean – I just have a couple of things –
  I need to – to wash my face, and – you know –

Phyllis Right – right, of course –
  All right –

  Phyllis hovers in the doorway for a moment, gazing at her daughter.
    Then she turns and leaves.
    Beat.
    Lori gets to her feet.
    She stands, surveying the room.
    She walks over to the window, bends down and switches on the fairy lights. She stands up and takes a step backwards and looks at them. She is impassive. She bends down again and switches them off. Then she slowly stands and takes them down from around the window, coiling them up carefully as she goes along. She sets the coil neatly on top of one of the boxes. She stands, staring at the room.

The living room.
 There is a cheerful fire blazing.
 David is standing watching it. Clover and Poppy are sitting close together. Poppy is cuddled up to Clover.

Phyllis (*coming into the room*) You've made a fire.

 She walks over to David. She leans against him.

Oh, love.

David (*quietly*) I know.

Poppy Isn't the fire nice?
 Just once won't hurt the ozone layer, will it, Dad.

Clover Is there anything we can do to help, Mum, 'cause anything you want us to do, isn't that right, Pops?

David Thank you, Clover. Poppy. You're good girls.

Phyllis (*to Clover*) Thank you, love.

Poppy (*getting up and cuddling into Phyllis*) Mum. Look at the funny shadows on the walls. Doesn't it make the room look like a different place.

 Phyllis puts an arm around Poppy.

David C'mere, Clover.

Clover What?

David 'Mere.

Clover (*reluctantly*) Da-ad –

 But she gets up and slouches over to her father.
 Silence.
 Poppy reaches for Clover's hand. Clover looks at her and squeezes her hand.
 Silence.

David We're going to be okay.

Silence.
  Then Lori comes into the room – bright – brittle – almost feverish.

Lori Anything I can do, come on Clovey, Pops. Clovey if you get the cutlery I'll get the glasses, wine, Mum, Dad, would you like a glass of wine, red or white, which would you prefer –

Slight silence.

Well go on, red or white, would you prefer / red or white –

David Red would be –

Phyllis There's a bottle of white open in the –

Lori Well, I'll get both, no problem, come on, Clovey –

She leaves the room. Phyllis and David glance quickly at each other; Clover and Poppy stare at each other; Poppy skips off first, beaming.

Poppy Come on, Clovey –

Clover Mum, do you think she's –

Poppy Come *on*, Clovey –

Poppy skips out of the room – the sound of laughter from the kitchen – she comes back with a stack of plates.

Clovey you're to get the cutlery – well, go *on* –

Clover leaves the room and comes back with the cutlery. The girls start setting the table; Lori comes back in with a glass of red and a glass of white wine and hands them to her parents.

Lori Here you go, Dad, Mum, here you go. Oh, doesn't it look pretty, I always think how pretty it looks, glasses and cutlery, before they're used, don't you, Mum, hey

Dad, will you sing a song, Dad, will you sing one of the songs you used to sing when we were little, will you?

Beat.

David A song?

Lori Yeah yeah, go on, please, Dad, one of the ones from when we were / little –

Clover A song?

Lori (*to Clover*) Yeah, wouldn't it be, I just thought it would be, hey Pops, you'd like a song, wouldn't you, go on, Dad. Pops, go get Dad's guitar –

Poppy leaps up to fetch the guitar.

David Lori, I haven't touched the guitar in months, it'll be / out of tune –

Lori Doesn't matter, you can tune it, that doesn't matter, go on, Dad –

Clover Lori –

Lori Aw, don't be a spoilsport – Clovey, come on, you'd like a song too, I know you would –

During the following speech Poppy comes scampering back with the guitar and hands it to her father, who puts his book down and takes the guitar and starts tuning. Lori jumps down cross-legged in front of him and Poppy cuddles in beside her; Clover hovers for a second and then sits down next to Phyllis, who puts an arm around her.

What are you going to sing, Dad, what do you think he'll sing, Clovey – 'mon and sit beside me, Pops, come on, isn't this nice, the fire's lovely, dead cosy, isn't it, Mum, oh that'll do, Dad, it's in tune enough by now, go on, go on –

*David starts to pluck out chords which resolve
themselves into a song; he begins to hum along softly
and then to sing. Lori whoops and claps when she
recognises it. Her enthusiasm is infectious: Poppy
cheers; Clover laughs despite herself; Phyllis smiles
too.*

David
Oh, I went down south to see my Sal
Singing Polly wolly doodle all the day
My Sal she am a spunky gal
Sing Polly wolly doodle all the day.

He pauses.

Lori Oh don't stop –

*She starts to hum the chorus, and David plays and
sings along:*

Fare thee well, fare thee well
Fare thee well my fairy Fay
For I'm off to Lou'siana for to see my Susyanna
Singing Polly wolly doodle all the day.

Then David alone:

Oh my Sal she is a maiden fair
Sing Polly wolly doodle all the day
With curly eyes and laughing hair
Sing Polly wolly doodle all the day.

Poppy Dad! The verse about the grasshopper, Dad!

David
Oh a grasshopper sittin' on a railroad track
Singing Polly wolly doodle all the day
A pickin' his teeth with a carpet tack
Sing Polly wolly doodle all the day.

Phyllis David?

I remember when you used to sing it to the girls before bedtime, and you'd sing *Poppy* wolly doodle.

Poppy Really?

Lori I remember that.

Poppy *Poppy* wolly doodle!

David is humming the chorus.

Lori (*suddenly not laughing*) I wish –

Clover (*quietly*) Shh, Lori, don't spoil it.

Phyllis What's that, Lori?

Lori Nothing.
I don't know what I was going to say.
Nothing.
I was just going to say that I wished –

Slight silence.

Phyllis (*gently*) What do you wish, Lori?

Poppy Yeah, what do you wish, Lori?

Lori I don't know, I can't –
What I mean is that –
I can't –

David It's going to be all right, Lori, everything's . . .

Lori (*suddenly, fiercely, to no one*) I'd give anything – anything – to start again. Anything. I mean if I believed in God, or in the Devil, or –
I'd give anything –

She stops, abruptly.
Nobody knows what to say.
Silence.
Slow fade to blackout.

Act Three

Three months earlier.
  The garden.
  It is early autumn. The evening is beginning to draw in;
it is nearing dusk, but is not yet dark. The day has been
crisp and bright; the sky is high and cloudless and, to the
west, is streaked with pink, like the traces of washed-out
blood. The leaves on the trees are a riot of reds and
oranges. There is a chill to the air, but it is not yet too
cold to sit outside. There is smart but faded wooden
garden furniture out: a table, chairs, etc. Lori is sitting at
the table alone, gazing at Clover and Poppy, who are
crouching on the ground giggling over two antique storm
lanterns which they are trying to light. There is a small
pile of gaudily wrapped presents on the table.
  Phyllis comes out from the kitchen, awkwardly (one-
handedly) untying an apron. She is carrying some
battered-looking jotters. She stops, and looks at Lori.
  Beat.

Phyllis Car all loaded up then?

  Beat.

Lori?

Lori What?

Phyllis Away with the fairies, you are.
  I said the car's all loaded up?

Lori Oh. Yeah.
  Dad's just – checking the oil and that.

Phyllis Right.

Slight silence.

(Are you) okay?

Lori What?
Yeah yeah. (*Slightly forced laugh.*) Yeah, I'm grand.
Just, you know.

Phyllis I know.

Beat.

(*Suddenly.*) Oh pet, I wish we were taking you over
ourselves.
Make sure you get there.
Don't go – astray, somehow.

Lori (*rallying*)
Mum. I'll be fine.
Dad's installed some sort of satellite navigation thingy
anyway that he says will tell me what street to take and
everything.
There'll be no way I can get lost even if I want to.
I'll be fine.

Phyllis It's just such a long drive. And the closer it gets to
you actually leaving –

Lori Mum.

Phyllis Sorry. I know, sorry.

Silence.

If there'd been someone who could have looked after your
sisters for the weekend, then your father and I would
by all means have taken you across – you do know that,
don't you.

Lori Mum.
We've been over all this.

Phyllis I know, but –

Lori Mum –

Phyllis I know, I know.

Beat.

Anyway, it'll be handy for you having your own car over there.

Lori Yeah.

Phyllis Just remember to use the wheel-lock, won't you? London isn't Belfast, you know.

Lori Mum.

Phyllis (*laughing faintly*) All right.
  Just –
  I still think of you as my baby, you know.

Lori But I'm not. And – and, Mum, Clover and Poppy aren't, either, you know.

Clover (*calling over*) I'll be the oldest now that Lori's gone.

Poppy Oh but that's not fair, it means I'm always the youngest –

Phyllis (*joking*)
  But don't you want to stay my baby, Poppy?

Poppy (*wriggling*) Yeah, but –

Phyllis I'm only joking, love. I'm only joking. No time at all it'll be you going away, too.

Silence.
  Clover manages to light the second of the lanterns.
  She picks it up carefully, and sets it on the table.

Clover There!
  Look, Mum!

Poppy goes to pick up the other lantern, which is also lit.

Careful, Pops –

Poppy I am *being* careful –

*Poppy sets the other lantern on the table.
She sits down.*

Clover (*sitting down*) They look pretty, don't they, Mum.

Phyllis (*sitting down*) Very pretty.

Beat.

Look, Lori – (*The jotters.*) Look what I found. I've been saving them to show you.

Lori What are they? (*Reading the cover.*) 'Dolores Murdoch Aged Seven And Three Quarters.' Ohh (*A sigh.*)

Poppy What is it? Let's see!

Lori (*softly*) Oh my *goodness* –

Phyllis And this one – look at this, Lori –
Wait a second till I –
Here we go, listen to this:
'Yesterday we went to the Botanic Gardens –' the teacher's written that bit in – 'Botanic Gardens' – 'and we saw a pheasant. Daddy said it was a pleasant pheasant.'
(*She laughs.*) 'Daddy said it was a pleasant pheasant.'

Lori I had no idea you kept them.

Phyllis Oh, everything's in the attic, somewhere or other.
Listen – listen to this – (*She flicks forward a few pages.*)
'Yesterday I helped Mummy give my baby sister a bath' – that's you, Poppy –

Poppy Me!

Phyllis (*continuing*) 'My baby sister has a bath every night.'

'Clover and I have a bath once a week on a Saturday night.'

'Clover and I have a bath once a week on a Saturday night' indeed!

You don't say that you had a shower every other night of the week! That bathtimes were a treat because you'd've stayed in there all night if we'd let you!

Clover Oh Lori, remember Mister Matey! Remember how we used to make tunnels in the bubbles!

Phyllis The two of youse splashing around like wee seals.

Poppy Did I splash around like a wee seal too?

Phyllis I used to bathe you in a baby-bath in the kitchen. Your sisters would wash their dolls in the sink at the same time.

Poppy Is that true?

Phyllis Oh, absolutely.

Lori (*reading over her mother's shoulder*) 'Once a week on a Saturday night.' Did I really write that?

Phyllis You did indeed. 'Once a week!' Whatever must the teacher have thought of us!

Beat.
She closes the jotter.

There's a whole box of them up there.

Silly keeping them, I know, but I just could never bring myself to throw them away.

Poppy Are all my primary school ones there too, Mum?

Clover Poppy, you only left primary school a couple of months ago!

Poppy Shut up!

Phyllis There are boxes and boxes of them. Your jotters, your drawings, your – I don't know – your music certificates, skating certificates, school reports –

Lori (*still flicking through the jotter*) God, Mum.

They lapse briefly into silence.
Then David comes out brandishing a bottle of champagne and glasses.

David Ta-daa!
All done, Lori.
And now –

Lori Champagne!
Dad!

Lori leaps up and hugs her father around the waist. He puts an arm around her.

Poppy We've been looking at Lori's old school jotters, Dad. From when she was, like, in P1 and that.

David You have, have you?

Poppy Mum found them in the attic. Lori, read Dad the bit about the pleasant pheasant!

Lori Later, Pops.

Poppy Why not now?

Lori Later.

Clover (*aside*) Lori doesn't want to, Poppy.

Poppy (*aside*) Why?

Clover (*shrugs*) I don't know. Just.

David So, who's for some bubbly, then?

Lori Dad you shouldn't've got *champagne*.

David But this is a very special occasion. I'd say there was cause for celebration, wouldn't you, Phyllis?

Phyllis Absolutely.

Lori (*joking*) What, so are we celebrating my going? Are you that pleased to be getting rid of me?

David Of course not, love.

Phyllis Oh but we are!

Lori Mum!

David Your mother's only joking, Lori.

Phyllis (*earnestly*) But we *are* pleased that you're going. You're making a new life for yourself, Lori, and this is the first step. And we're proud of you for working so hard, and for getting so far, and –

Lori Mu-um –

Phyllis (*continuing*) – no, but we are, Lori, and it's brave of you: tell me, how many from your year are going across the water?

Clover Hardly anyone in Lori's year, isn't that right, Lori?

Lori A few are going across to Scotland –

Clover Yeah but most of them are staying here, aren't they, Lori.
I can't wait to come and visit you.

Poppy Me too! Mum, can I go across and visit Lori at Hallowe'en?

Phyllis We'll see.

Poppy No, but can I?

Clover I want to go over first.

You're probably too young, Poppy, like for the student bars and all –

Phyllis (*laughing*) And you're not, Clover?

Clover No, but that's different, Mum –

David Girls, girls, girls –
Lori's going to be settling in, and making new friends, and studying hard – she might not want to see you so soon –

Clover Oh but she will, won't you, Lori –

David Well, we'll see.
The terms aren't that long – she'll be back here in no time at all.

Phyllis She hasn't even got there yet, David, and already you're talking about her coming back home.

Beat.

We are proud of you, Lori.
We are all very proud of you.

Beat.

David Well are we going to drink this or not?
Lori, are you going to open it?

Lori You do it, Dad.

Lori lines the glasses up.
David opens the bottle of champagne.
Clover and Poppy clap and cheer, and Phyllis laughs.
Lori smiles.
David pours three full glasses, and two half-full glasses, and Lori hands them around.

David To Lori.

Phyllis / Clover / Poppy To Lori!

Phyllis To our little daughter all grown up / and about to –

David Oh, Phyllis, you're embarrassing her.
  To our daughter.

They clink glasses and drink.

Clover Look at Poppy!

Poppy (*grimacing*) The bubbles went up my nose!

They laugh.
  Happy pause as they sip at their drinks.
  After a bit David gets up and wanders across the garden, still holding his glass of champagne, and inspects the base of the fence.
  A moment later Poppy jumps up after him and scuffs at some of the leaves on the lawn.

Phyllis I was going to say let's eat outside one last time but I think it's getting too cold.

Lori Let's sit out a bit longer. The garden looks so pretty. The leaves on the trees.

Silence.
  Phyllis starts flicking through the jotters.

Poppy (*calling to her father*) Remember you used to rake up big piles of leaves and we all used to jump in them?

David (*calling back*) Have a bonfire soon.

Beat.

Lori (*suddenly; to herself*)
  Come little leaves, said the wind one day,
  Come to the meadows with me and play
  Put on your dresses of red and gold
  Summer is gone and the days grow cold.

Clover What?

Lori What?

Clover What's that?

Lori Oh. Just an old rhyme. I was trying to remember how it goes. I can't remember the rest.

Clover Say it again.

Lori It's silly. And I can't remember how the rest of it goes.

Clover Mum, do you remember?
Mum?

Phyllis What's that, love?

Clover 'Come little leaves –' Say the rest of it, Lori – it's like a nursery rhyme or something –

Phyllis I don't think so. There were so many rhymes we used to sing to you.

Beat.

If you looked through some of the books in the attic, maybe.

Silence. She closes the jotters.

Well.

Beat.
She looks around her. Calling suddenly:

More champagne, David?

David turns and walks back over to the table. Poppy skips behind him. He stands behind Lori and rests a hand lightly on her shoulder. Phyllis tops up all of the glasses except for Poppy's.

Poppy Oh Mum, can I not have some more too?

Phyllis Poppy . . .

David Go on, Phyl. / Special occasion and all that.

Clover Dad, Mum *hates* it when you call her Phyl –

David (*chuckling suddenly*) Her nickname in school was the Philosopher.

Clover Really?
  Mum? Is that true?

David She was always near the top of the year.

Phyllis *Near* the top?

David I do beg your pardon – she was always top.
  Well, mostly, anyhow.
  She used to help me with my science homework.
  Isn't that right, Philosopher?

Phyllis Your father pretending to be terrible at science so that he'd have an excuse to talk to me.

  She laughs and shakes her head and splashes some champagne into Poppy's glass.

David Just this once, eh, Poppy?

Poppy Da-ad.

  Beat.

Presents! Let's do the presents now!

Phyllis (*laughing*) All right, Poppy.

  David sits down and smiles at his wife.
    Poppy selects a present from the pile and hands it ceremoniously to Lori.
    Lori unwraps it. It is a student cookbook.

Lori (*laughing*) Mu-um –

Phyllis (*laughing*) I don't want to think of you surviving on – I don't know, Pot Noodles.

And I've baked you a cake, it's just cooling on the rack inside –

Lori Oh Mum –

Phyllis Lemon drizzle. I'll put it in a tin and you can invite people back to your room for a slice.

Lori (*laughing*) What, a more innocent version of 'inviting them in for a coffee'? / In case 'coffee' sounds too obvious?

Phyllis (*laughing; slightly feigning shock*) Dolores Murdoch!

You know fine well / that is not –

Lori I know, / I know –

Phyllis (*suddenly not laughing*) I just thought –

Lori (*not laughing*) I know.
It's a lovely thought.
Thanks, Mum.

Phyllis Give her another present, Poppy.

Poppy hands Lori another present. It is a hot-water bottle with a fleecy cover.

Lori (*laughing and holding it up*) Oh Mum –

Phyllis Well.
At least I know you'll be warm and fed.

Beat.

Poppy!

Poppy selects an oddly shaped package. She does not know what it is. She looks at her mother questioningly. Phyllis shrugs and turns to David. Lori shakes and pokes it in exaggerated amusement. Then she opens it. It is a packet of Tayto crisps.

Lori (*laughing hard*) Dad –

Phyllis (*laughing*) David, what on earth –

They are all laughing.

David Good Ulster crisps. In case you get homesick. You don't get Tayto over in England.

Phyllis (*laughing*) David –

Clover seizes a present and gives it to Lori.

Clover And this is from me. (*It is a homemade CD.*) I put some of your favourite songs on it.
   And 'The Skaters' Waltz'.
   Remember 'The Skaters' Waltz'?

Lori 'The Skaters' Waltz'!
   Oh my goodness!
   I haven't heard that in –
   God.

Clover Yeah.
   I thought it would be – nice memories for you.

Lori Thank you.

Clover Except the only recording I found of it is a bit slow. I couldn't find the version we liked. It was – I don't know. Faster. Better. Well. The way I remember it anyway.

Phyllis We had it on tape, once. I wonder if it's still around anywhere. Probably not.
   'The Skaters' Waltz' was what made you want to learn to play music, Clover.

Clover Yeah.

Phyllis The DJ at the Ice Bowl played it at the end of Lori's birthday party. I asked him afterwards what the piece of music was called and bought the cassette. You played it over and over and begged and begged for music lessons.

Clover (*smiling*) Yeah.

Phyllis I always wondered where that came from. There's nobody particularly musical on my side of the family.

Lori Dad plays guitar.

Phyllis Yes. But you know what I mean.

    Beat.

Your twelfth birthday party. Imagine!

Lori That was the best birthday party ever.

Phyllis It doesn't seem like yesterday.
And now look at you!

Lori Yeah.

    Silence.

Thanks, Clovey.

Clover I'm going to miss you so much, Lori. So much.

    Beat.

Lori I know.

    Beat.

Poppy Lori, this one's from me!

    It is a garish and sparkly pink photograph album.
    Clover starts giggling behind her hand.
    Lori starts giggling too.

Why are you laughing?

Lori I'm not laughing, honestly –
  Oh, Poppy, it's so sweet of you.

Poppy You do like it? Promise you're not just saying
that? 'Cause Clover said to get the other one but *I* thought
you'd like this one better.

Lori I love it.
  Give me a kiss.

  Poppy jumps up and hugs Lori.

Poppy You have to take photos of *everyone* you meet
and *everything* you do. To show us when you come
home. And Mum wants to see what your boyfriends look
like.

Lori Mum!

  They laugh.

Poppy If we'd lived two hundred years ago you'd almost
be too old to get married, Lori. We'd all be worried
because Clovey and me couldn't get married until you
did, probably.

Lori Thanks for that, Pops.

Phyllis Where did that come from, Poppy?

Poppy History. We did it in school. It's true, though!

Phyllis Well, aren't you lucky times have changed.
  You girls – all of you girls –
  You have opportunities. You have –
  You can do anything.
  You can go anywhere.

Lori Mum.

Phyllis It's true, Lori. And you make the most of it.

  Beat.

Lori I'm nothing special, Mum.

Poppy You're special to us, Lori!
And I reckon she's special anyway, isn't she, Dad?

Lori Don't –
Look –
I was only saying.
Just let's –

Beat.

David Come on.
There's one more present here.

*The last present is large. Lori looks questioningly at
her father. He nods at her to go ahead. She stands up
and opens it. It is a laptop computer.*

You'll be needing one of those. All the work you'll be
doing.

Lori (*slightly flatly*) Wow, Dad –
God –
Wow. Thank you.
Wow.

David It's from your mother as well.

Lori Yeah of course – Mum –
Thank you.

David Leave it in the box. Keep it safe until you get there.

Lori Okay, yeah.

She closes the box over and sits down.

Thank you. I mean it.
All of you.
God, I'm going to cry or something –

David (*gently*) No you're not. You'll be back in no time.
No time at all.

They fall into silence.

Poppy (*suddenly*) I'm hungry. When's dinner?

Phyllis (*getting up*) Dinner'll be ready soon. Who's going to lay the table?

Silence.

Clover?

Clover Mu-um.
I think Lori should help. Seeing as she's not going to get a chance for weeks.

Phyllis (*glancing at Lori and David*) Oh Clover.
Let Lori stay and finish her champagne.
Come on, love. I'd appreciate a hand.

Clover gets up reluctantly.

Clover Is Poppy going to help, too?

Poppy I want to stay outside with Lori.

Phyllis Please, Clover –

Clover All right, all right, I'm coming.

Phyllis It's getting too dark to sit outside, anyhow.

Beat.

David, you will make sure you put out those lanterns before you come in?

David (*gently*) Of course.

Phyllis Right.
Good.

Silence.

Lori (*suddenly*) Mum –

Phyllis Lori?

Beat.

Lori Don't go in yet.
Just sit for a little bit?

Phyllis (*gently*) Lori, love, dinner will be spoiled –

Lori Please.
It's –
It's just nice, all of us.

*Beat. Phyllis sighs and sits down at the table. Clover
sits down, too.*
Nobody speaks. Dusk is falling.
Slow fade to blackout.